The devotions in *The Chosen* put us into the story of the ordinary people who surrounded Jesus. No plastic saints here, just sinners who spent time with the one Man who understood them and would eventually die for them. These are stories of rebuke and hope, of sin and forgiveness. Yes, their story is ours. Read *The Chosen* and pass it along to some other struggling sinners who need to see Jesus in a new light.

—Dr. Erwin Lutzer, pastor emeritus,
The Moody Church, Chicago, Illinois

I don't know of anyone like Dallas Jenkins. His fresh eyes and instincts take the greatest stories ever told and make them new. This beautiful and powerful devotional is borne of that same gift. You will be inspired and motivated to live life to the fullest as you read these deep insights!

—Pastor Ray Bentley, author, speaker, and
pastor of Maranatha Chapel, San Diego, California

In *The Chosen*, three voices join as one to lead you on a remarkable forty-day journey with Jesus. You'll meet the people who loved Him, served Him, and followed Him, seeing the Savior through their eyes as you consider who He is and why He came. The writing style is relatable and accessible, and the prayer focus for each devotion provides the perfect landing spot. And the questions meant to help you move forward in your faith are challenging enough to do just that. A gem of a book!

—LIZ CURTIS HIGGS, best-selling author of
Bad Girls of the Bible

THE
CHOSEN

40 DAYS WITH JESUS

By
Amanda Jenkins,
Kristen Hendricks,
& Dallas Jenkins

BroadStreet
PUBLISHING

BroadStreet Publishing® Group, LLC
Savage, Minnesota, USA
BroadStreetPublishing.com

THE CHOSEN: 40 Days with Jesus

978-1-4245-5785-1 (faux leather)
978-1-4245-5786-8 (e-book)

Stock or custom editions of BroadStreet Publishing titles may be purchased in bulk for educational, business, ministry, fundraising, or sales promotional use. For information, please email info@broadstreetpublishing.com.

Represented by Dan Balow at the Steve Laube Agency
Cover design by Chris Garborg at garborgdesign.com
Typesetting by Kjell Garborg at garborgdesign.com

Printed in China
19 20 21 22 23 5 4 3 2 1

To Simon Peter, Mary Magdalene,
Nicodemus, and Matthew.
Before they were heroes of the faith
who inspired *The Chosen* series,
they were desperate sinners like us.

CONTENTS

FOREWORD

When the Son of God walked the earth in our shoes, He connected with humanity through story. Jesus used our own tales to help us understand God's truths. He communicated the immutable principles of the heavens with parables of familiar, earthly circumstances and relatable characters to which any of His listeners could universally identify. They were anecdotes, chronicles, and narratives that became like soul food to everyone He met.

That's how God the Father has been giving His revelation to humankind since the dawn of the cosmos. Through story, because God is and has always been the First Author: "In the beginning was the Word, and the Word was with God, and the Word was God" (John 1:1, emphasis added).

God knows that when we are most hungry spiritually, the themes of heaven—grace, forgiveness, sacrifice, redemption, reconciliation, and resurrection—will resonate in our hearts and draw us closer to Him. Those themes are like violin strings running through our souls and, when plucked in just the right way, always reverberate back the plumb line of God's truth.

That is what my friend, Dallas Jenkins, is creating with his powerful media series, *The Chosen*, which takes us on a journey with Jesus through the eyes of the real people whose lives He absolutely transformed with His words, love, and deeds. Imagine what it would be like to walk the dusty roads of those characters who encountered the Messiah.

That is what you are going to find in these beautiful and powerful devotions. Take *The Chosen* journey these next forty days. Read and reflect on these devotions. Digest them as food for your soul. And then write them in your heart, not with ink, but with the Spirit of the living God.

Brian Bird

Screenwriter and producer of *The Case for Christ* film and television series *When Calls the Heart*; co-author of the devotional series *When God Calls the Heart*

FROM THE DIRECTOR
OF *THE CHOSEN*

I've been a believer my whole life, I've attended Christian schools my whole life, and I've heard the stories of Jesus countless times. I've also seen every Jesus movie and miniseries ever made, and there have been dozens. So why a new TV show about Jesus?

Because of what you're reading now.

I have a passion for people to hear the "old, old story" again … for the very first time. When I see Jesus movies, it's very rare for me to be moved or excited, and the same is true for a lot of Jesus-related devotionals. Quite frankly, I've heard it all before, and it's hard to relate to the perfect and sinless Son of God. However, I *can* relate to the sinners who surrounded Him. Problem is, most Jesus projects just take you from Bible story to Bible story, glossing over the humanity and backstories of all these characters.

So when I started creating a TV show that explores Jesus through the eyes of the people around Him, I found myself getting moved and excited. I was experiencing Him in the way they did, and the reaction to the Christmas special pilot episode about the birth of Christ from the perspective of the shepherds confirmed we were on to something. We kept hearing, "I've heard this before but never in this way."

As we wrote episodes and this devotional, we explored the backstories of Simon Peter, Matthew, Mary Magdalene, Nicodemus, and a few of Jesus' miracle recipients. We couldn't help but identify with their recklessness, rough past, religious piety, and desperation for life change … and ultimately, their redemption.

Again, why a new TV show about Jesus?

So that we can go deeper, and hopefully this book will help with that. None of this matters if it doesn't compel you back to Scripture—not only so you can experience Jesus the way His followers did, but also so you can *change* and *grow* the way they did.

So please, if you've chosen (no pun intended) to dig into this material with us, make full use of it. Jesus' followers were students (it's why they called Him "Rabbi" and "Teacher"). Be a student. Write stuff down, pray on what you're reading and writing, and celebrate the fact that you're chosen to be an ambassador for the one who created the world.

Let me be clear: The project in front of you is connected to the TV show, yes, but only in the sense that we're compelled to show *and* tell in order to revive your passion for Scripture and the one who inspired it. We hope watching the show enhances your experience with this book, and we hope engaging with this book enhances your experience watching the show. But we didn't create this to capitalize on the show; you'll see plenty in here that isn't covered in our episodes. This would exist even if the show didn't.

I don't know what stage you're at in your journey with Christ—whether you're a Mary Magdalene who encountered Jesus after a horrific past without Him … or you're a Nicodemus who's been a lifelong member of the God team. But as Jesus proved over and over, we've got tons to learn and innumerable traits that need change. Thanks for taking that journey with us.

Dallas Jenkins
Director, *The Chosen*

BEFORE

"Fear not, for I have redeemed you;
I have called you by name, you are mine."

Isaiah 43:1

Every follower of Jesus has a not-so-great "before": A rash, brash fisherman. A pious, fancy-pants religious leader. A thieving, indifferent-to-suffering tax collector. A demon-possessed woman so insignificant that her "before" isn't even recorded and we're left to surmise what it might've been.

And yet God calls people in the "before"—when they aren't even aware they're simply broken versions of themselves. God calls people *before* He begins His transformative work of redemption because He sees past the "before" to what He purposed and planned. He sees past the "before" to those He loves enough to call His own.

Take Israel, for example.

Isaiah prophesied over God's chosen nation—"Fear not, for I have redeemed you" (Isaiah 43:1)—not during a time of obedience but during their rebellion. A time filled with idol worship and wandering hearts and intense callousness to sin, not to mention all the painful consequences they were experiencing as a result of their choices. It was spoken long before their repentance.

"I have called you by name, you are mine," he continues in verse 1. When Isaiah spoke those words, Israel was rebelling against all God had done for them and all He wanted to do. But God didn't turn away—He showed mercy. He spoke His love over His chosen people, claiming them as His own before they agreed to be.

He entered into the "before."

God speaks what is true over us too; His plan of redemption is on the march, because He has called us by name. Our choices don't derail His. What we see when we look in the mirror doesn't determine what He sees or who we'll be by His hand, and so our brokenness doesn't alter His plans. Nor do circumstances, other people, or our own choices determine our value; our value is assigned by the one we belong to.

So we don't have to fear.

Fear not, you're not who you're going to be. Fear not, God can redeem your choices and use them for good. Fear not, God can heal your heart, your body, your relationships. Fear not, you were made for more than what you've experienced so far. Fear not, this is only the beginning.

Every follower of Jesus has a not-so-great "before." But every follower of Jesus also has an "after." The rowdy fisherman became the bedrock preacher of the early church, healer of the sick and lame, and fearless unto death. The leader of impersonal religion became personal friends with Jesus, finally understanding and being changed by the Scriptures he'd devoted his life to studying. The taxman traitor became a member of the elite twelve and author of the first Gospel of the New Testament. And the woman? The woman too insignificant to even have her "before" recorded was so precious to Jesus that she became the first person He appeared to after He rose from the dead, the first one to hear His tender voice, and the first witness of the culmination of all He claimed to be and do—and she got to tell the boys.

PRAYER FOCUS

Thank the Father for knowing your name and calling it—and for identifying you as His. Thank Him for redeeming you from your "before," then ask Him to help you through any remaining challenges.

MOVING FORWARD

o What parts of your "before" has God redeemed, and which are you most grateful for?

o How does "I have called you by name, you are mine" impact you today?

o What do you fear, and how does Isaiah 43:1—this declaration made by God to His chosen ones—affect your fear?

DELIVERED

"The LORD is my rock and my fortress
and my deliverer."

2 SAMUEL 22:2

We've all been delivered from things. Our mothers delivered us from their wombs. Good explanations delivered us from confusion. Time delivers us from our pasts.

It's a continual process, deliverance. It comes in all shapes and forms and ranges from significant events to the familiar moments that slip by quietly. Mary Magdalene knew this well.

First, she was delivered from seven demons. Then, over the course of Jesus' three years of ministry, she was delivered from everything she thought she knew. Mary went from being constantly tormented by darkness

(Luke 8:2) to being regularly enlightened by the Light of the World, Jesus. The sparse details about her life prior to Christ only serve to emphasize her deliverance—meaning that because Jesus delivered her from death, she followed Him to His. Mary Magdalene was one of the few with Jesus until the very end.

Familiarity developed over that three-year span of ministry. She knew His voice and His laugh. She listened intently to His teaching. Some of His words she could process immediately, some she failed to fully comprehend. She marveled at Jesus' compassion for the suffering and marginalized. She became fiercely loyal to the one who healed the oppressed and set captives free. Each subsequent miracle substantiated what she knew the moment she experienced her own: He was the Messiah.

Jesus was arrested. The disciples scattered. And Mary found herself standing at the foot of the cross with the woman who had delivered the Messiah into the world.

After His crucifixion, Mary Magdalene went to the tomb and saw that the stone had been rolled away. Jesus—the Messiah, her deliverer, teacher, and friend—was not there. The Gospels have varying accounts of what happens next, but Luke 24 says she was reminded of what Jesus had told her in Galilee: "The Son of Man must be delivered over to the hands of sinners, be crucified and on the third day be raised again" (v.7 NIV). Those words had eluded her before, but now she remembered and understood that He too was delivered.

After the ultimate sacrifice, the resurrected Christ appeared first to this devoted woman we know so little about. But Jesus knew her. He knew exactly what He had delivered her from and for. And while standing in front of the empty tomb, Jesus told her it was her turn. Mary Magdalene would be the first to deliver the single most important message in human history: He has risen!

PRAYER FOCUS

Thank God for the fact that His deliverance allowed for yours, then ask Him for guidance in delivering the news to others.

MOVING FORWARD

o Describe what Christ has delivered you *from*.

o In what ways can you identify with Mary Magdalene?

o What role has Christ delivered you *for*?

REPRESENT

"If anyone would come after me, let [her] deny
[herself] and take up [her] cross daily and follow me.
For whoever would save [her] life will lose it,
but whoever loses [her] life for my sake will save it."

Luke 9:23–24

To save our lives, we must lose them. That's a mind
bender, for sure, but clearly vital to understand. Jesus
said it to the disciples after they'd already dropped
everything to follow Him from town to town. They
sacrificed their careers, homes, and relationships for the
man they believed was the Messiah. Life as they knew it
had turned upside down, but more would be required
of them, and Jesus was doubling down. He knew what
lay ahead. He knew He was leaving. And He knew they
would become pillars of the early church, in charge

of spreading the truth about salvation to the world, discipling the masses, and claiming Christ in the face of imprisonment, torture, and death. They would lose their lives on earth—figuratively and literally—for the sake of all they would gain in heaven.

And they did it well because their testimonies, their personal stories of what Jesus had said and done, were potent demonstrations of His transformative love and power in their lives. They shared the gospel with an unstoppable, contagious, relentless passion that—to be honest—seems kind of rare these days.

How come?

Well for starters, they weren't in love with themselves or their own stories. They weren't branding their Christian narratives for maximum personal benefit, approval, or sympathy … or for clicks or likes. They weren't assigning themselves the hero role or belaboring their "before Christ" dysfunction with all its juicy, sensationalistic tidbits. When you look at biblical examples, it's amazing how few words are given to their broken pasts—the almost exclusive focus is on Jesus.

Take Mary Magdalene. The fact that she was delivered from seven demons is a crucial aspect of her testimony because it showcases Jesus' authority and why she responded to Him the way she did. And then that's it. That's all the detail we need to know. In other words, her autobiography wouldn't have been titled *The Dark*

Years with three hundred pages dedicated to describing the monsters within. Fascinating? Sure. But powerful and effective and glorifying to the one who rescued her? Not so much. There's a reason we meet Mary subsequent to her healing—because that's where the real story is.

There are a few other things we know about her: (1) she followed Jesus and financially supported His ministry until His crucifixion, which means she gave everything she had to follow Him; (2) she endured the crucifixion and stayed close to Jesus while He suffered and died; and (3) as mentioned in "Delivered," she was the first person He appeared to after He rose from the dead, and she was the one He sent to tell the disciples the universe-altering news. All because the old was gone and dead. Jesus had given her new life.

Which means that even if you've been a believer for all of ten minutes, those minutes are entirely more relevant than the twenty, forty, or eighty years of darkness prior to your conversion. Reason being, we're called to represent Jesus and to die to the lives He saved us from. When we do that, and when He stays the hero of the story, our words and lives become real-time, potent demonstrations of His transformative love and power.

PRAYER FOCUS

Thank God for how He's transformed you, repent of any times you've represented Jesus poorly, and ask Him to be part of how you tell your story.

MOVING FORWARD

o Do you find it difficult to share your testimony? Why or why not?

o Be real: Who or what do your words most represent?

o Moving forward, what can you say that focuses more on the "after Christ" portion of your testimony than the "before Christ" portion?

WORDS

In the beginning was the Word, and the Word was with
God, and the Word was God. He was in the beginning
with God. All things were made through him, and
without him was not any thing made that was made.
In him was life, and the life was the light of men.
The light shines in the darkness, and the darkness
has not overcome it.

John 1:1–5

The Word was in the beginning, before the heavens and
earth, before sunsets and the Pacific, before wildflowers
and whales and strawberries and freckles. He was before
all of it because He made all of it. The Word spoke the
world into existence, which is perhaps why Jesus was
called the Word. By His words came all that we know,
and by His words come light and knowledge, healing

and hope. The words Jesus spoke changed the course of history—along with the lives of twelve very ordinary men.

The disciples were an unconventional group made up largely of fishermen, an anarchist Zealot, and a thieving tax collector—none of whom would've scored very high on a likeability scale. They were rough around the edges and ranged from salt-of-the-earth and smelly to downright sketchy. They were loud, proud, greedy, defensive, skeptical, and independent, or some combination thereof, so it's a wonder such men wholly responded to Jesus' simple words in Mark 1:17: "Follow me."

> Passing alongside the Sea of Galilee, he saw Simon and Andrew the brother of Simon casting a net into the sea, for they were fishermen. And Jesus said to them, "Follow me, and I will make you become fishers of men." And immediately they left their nets and followed him. And going on a little farther, he saw James the son of Zebedee and John his brother, who were in their boat mending the nets. And immediately he called them, and they left their father Zebedee in the boat with the hired servants and followed him. (vv. 16–20)

What in the world! They dropped everything and followed Him, just like that? We get a little more context regarding Simon Peter and Andrew in Luke 5:1–11. Jesus had performed a miracle just before His audacious request. But still, it was crazy talk. So I have to imagine the words sounded different from Jesus than they would've from anyone else—anyone other than The Word. "In him was life, and the life was the light of men. The light shines in the darkness, and the darkness has not overcome it" (John 1:4–5).

As strange as it is to imagine dropping everything familiar for what is entirely unknown, somehow the trade made sense. In Jesus is life, so His words transcend circumstances and break down barriers. They light up dark corners, removing fear, doubt, and self-preservation. They bring clarity and elevate our understanding of what's real, true, and important. They take us from completely missing our purpose to seeing in neon that our only reason for being is to follow the one who spoke us into being.

The disciples gave up all they had to follow Jesus when He called them. For three years they sat under His teaching and listened to Him pray. They watched Him welcome children and honor the least of these. They heard Him tell jokes, laugh at their jokes, and be respectful to His mom. They witnessed Him heal the sick, defend His Father's house, and chastise the self-righteous. With words.

And they stood helpless when He said no words on His way to the cross. So of course twelve ordinary men, initially full of hot air and void of purpose, became the very ones so changed by Jesus' words that they would fearlessly take them to the ends of the earth.

PRAYER FOCUS

Thank the Father for whatever words impacted your life most, such as your favorite Bible verse. And recommit to Him to read His Word and say His words to others.

MOVING FORWARD

o Describe your first "Follow me" moment with Jesus.

o Which words of Jesus do you cherish most?

o How can you make your own words (particularly on social media) more like Christ's words?

RENEGADE

The true light, which gives light to everyone, was coming into the world. He was in the world, and the world was made through him, yet the world did not know him. He came to his own, and his own people did not receive him. But to all who did receive him, who believed in his name, he gave the right to become children of God, who were born, not of blood nor of the will of the flesh nor of the will of man, but of God.

JOHN 1:9–13

He was coming. Like in a movie.

It's the premise of a lot of great westerns: At a desolate time in a desolate place, the stage is set for an unlikely hero to emerge; only instead of the gun-slinging cowboy riding in to save the town (and the dame—wrong genre), it was Jesus, and He was coming to save the world.

But the world did not know Him.

Think of that. Creator God walked among His creation for the purpose of saving them, and they had no clue. But why would they? First, He was too average looking to be noticed: "He had no form or majesty that we should look at him, and no beauty that we should desire him" (Isaiah 53:2). Second, He was too poor to be impressive. According to the Law, a lamb was the required sacrifice for atonement of sin unless someone was too poor to afford one, in which case two doves or pigeons could be offered instead: "And when the time came for [Mary and Joseph's] purification according to the Law of Moses, they brought [Jesus] up to Jerusalem to present him to the Lord … and to offer a sacrifice according to what is said in the Law of the Lord, 'a pair of turtledoves, or two young pigeons'" (Luke 2:22, 24). Third, He was from Nazareth, a town so small and off the beaten path that it was considered uneducated, backwoods, full of hicks and sticks: "Philip found Nathanael and said to him, 'We have found him of whom Moses in the Law and also the prophets wrote, Jesus of Nazareth, the son of Joseph.' Nathanael said to him, 'Can anything good come out of Nazareth?'" (John 1:45–46).

He came to His own, and they did not receive Him.

Jesus was raised in Nazareth, but He didn't stay there. When He claimed to be the Messiah, they rejected Him—then they ran Him outta town on a rail. "When [the people of Nazareth] heard these things, all in the synagogue were filled with wrath. And they rose up and drove [Jesus] out of the town and brought him to the brow of the hill on which their town was built, so that they could throw him down the cliff. But passing through their midst, he went away" (Luke 4:28–30).

But to all who received Him …

To *all*. Besides faith, there were no requirements for having a relationship with Jesus. No status, no age, no race, no gender. No prior education or track record of good behavior—the greater the transgression, the greater the forgiveness. He welcomed the poor, the rich, the intelligent, and the not-so-much. He, in fact, broke every cultural, political, and social boundary in pursuit of the all: "There is neither Jew nor Greek, there is neither slave nor free, there is no male and female, for you are all one in Christ Jesus" (Galatians 3:28).

He gave the right to become children of God.

Through Jesus, we lay claim to heaven's territory, its rights and its riches. Jesus becomes our brother and God our Father. "But as it is, they desire a better country, that is, a heavenly one. Therefore God is not ashamed to be called their God, for he has prepared for them a city" (Hebrews 11:16).

So yeah, it was tough to recognize Jesus as the Messiah, the Hero, especially because of what He looked like, how He acted, and who He chose to spend time with. But those who got it, those who followed the renegade once their eyes were opened—they reaped the reward. And so can we. And with Him we become our own kind of renegade—with Jesus, ride or die.

PRAYER FOCUS

Worship the Father and Son for their unique characteristics, and ask God to give you strength and courage to proudly proclaim you follow a renegade.

MOVING FORWARD

- o What is most striking to you about the way Jesus began His ministry years?

- o Jesus repeatedly extended His hand to all types of people. In what ways do you need to be more like Him? Who do you struggle to welcome?

- o In what ways are you a renegade for Jesus? In what ways do you need to become more of one?

REDEMPTION

The law was given through Moses; grace and truth
came through Jesus Christ. No one has ever seen
God; the only God, who is at the Father's side, he has
made him known.

JOHN 1:17–18

The Old Testament is full of strange things: stories of
a man-swallowing fish, a flood that rebooted the earth,
a brass section that brought down the walls of a city—
just to name a few. And there are plenty more where
that crazy came from. Some stories are so outside the
norm, they're difficult to imagine. And sometimes it's
even more difficult to discern God's purpose behind
them, at least at first glance, which is why reading about
Jesus is such a gift. So much of what God did in the Old

Testament makes sense when we learn about the things Jesus did and said in the New.

Take the fish. God wanted to save the sinful, broken people of Nineveh, but His spokesman didn't want the job. Instead of letting Jonah sail in the opposite direction, God had him thrown off the boat and swallowed by a sea monster that promptly swam back to Nineveh. For three days and nights, Jonah was in the belly of the beast—the same amount of time Jesus was in the tomb. Once "resurrected" (i.e., barfed onto shore), Jonah delivered God's message of repentance and redemption—and the Ninevites believed. Nineveh's salvation story was a picture, a foreshadowing of what would take place on the cross: (1) humanity rebelled against God, (2) God made a miraculous way for righteousness to be restored, and (3) God gave grace to the people who believed.

Then there's Noah. God told him to build the biggest boat anyone had ever seen, one so ginormous that it couldn't have been towed from the building site to the dock; water would have to come to it. And Noah endured relentless mocking from all the God rejectors who were watching—that is, until the rain came, flooding the earth and wiping out every living thing *not* on that boat. Noah's salvation story was a picture, a foreshadowing of what would take place on the cross: (1) humanity rebelled against God, (2) God made a miraculous way for righteousness to be restored, and (3) God gave grace to the (eight) people who believed.

And let's not forget Jericho, a fortified city that stood between the Israelites and the land God had promised them. God told the Israelites to conquer Jericho by marching around its perimeter wall for seven days while blowing trumpets—perhaps the least intimidating of all the horns, but I digress. On the seventh day, God brought the walls of the city crumbling down, killing everyone inside except a small remnant of believers. Once again, Israel's salvation story was a picture, a foreshadowing of what would take place on the cross: (1) humanity rebelled against God, (2) God made a miraculous way for righteousness to be restored, and (3) God gave grace to those who believed.

That 1-2-3 pattern can be seen in the majority of Old Testament stories, but the supernatural bells and whistles sometimes keep us from seeing the heart of the matter—that from earth's first moment until now, and from now until the end of the world as we know it, God is writing a story of rescue and redemption. And Jesus—the Creator of the world, the one who whispers to clouds to make them pour out snow, the one who sculpted Mount Everest and dug out the Grand Canyon, the one who mapped out the galaxy and hung every star—wrote Himself into that story. He allowed himself, in human form, to (1) be rebelled against, (2) provide a miraculous way for humanity to be restored, and (3) give grace to all who believe.

And because Jesus restored us, showing us who God was and what He was doing, we can learn from the Old Testament, but we no longer have to repeat it. "No one has ever seen God; the only God, who is at the Father's side, [Jesus] has made him known" (John 1:18).

PRAYER FOCUS

Thank God for His story of redemption, then ask Him to reveal Himself even more in all the ways you're pursuing Him.

MOVING FORWARD

o What was the point of God's 1-2-3 pattern in the Old Testament?

o What does His sacrifice on the cross reveal to you about God the Father?

o How can you live out gratitude for the grace you've already been given for your rebellion?

DOUBT

And there appeared to [Zechariah] an angel of the Lord standing on the right side of the altar of incense. And Zechariah was troubled when he saw him, and fear fell upon him. But the angel said to him, "Do not be afraid, Zechariah, for your prayer has been heard, and your wife Elizabeth will bear you a son, and you shall call his name John. And you will have joy and gladness, and many will rejoice at his birth, for he will be great before the Lord … And Zechariah said to the angel, "How shall I know this? For I am an old man, and my wife is advanced in years." And the angel answered him, "I am Gabriel. I stand in the presence of God, and I was sent to speak to you and to bring you this good news. And behold, you will be silent and unable to speak until the day that these things take place, because you did not believe my words, which will be fulfilled in their time."

LUKE 1:11–15, 18–20

Reporter: Zechariah, you've been a priest for many years. It's been said that you and your wife, Elizabeth, are righteous in the sight of God and observe His commands and decrees blamelessly. So … why was it such a struggle to believe Gabriel when he announced that you would have a son?

Zechariah: First of all, having an angel appear before you is utterly terrifying. Furthermore, I was in the temple on official business performing my priestly duty. The last thing I expected was a personal encounter with the archangel Gabriel.

Reporter: So your doubt was due to the personal nature of the message?

Zechariah: Of course. It took me off guard. Not to mention Elizabeth and I were already old, well beyond childbearing age.

Reporter: You didn't recall the story of Abraham and Sarah … or Hannah or Rebekah or Rachel … or other barren women with whom God miraculously intervened?

Zechariah: What I recalled was how much we had prayed for a child. For many years Elizabeth and I petitioned God. We prayed with great faith. We hoped. We trusted. For decades, we did this.

Reporter: And nothing happened.

Zechariah: And nothing happened. Then it was too late, and with heavy hearts we accepted it was God's will.

Reporter: Did Gabriel's announcement feel more painful than hopeful?

Zechariah: Hope can be painful, or so I thought. Gabriel said my prayer had been heard. He told me Elizabeth would bear a son and we were to call him John. That he would be a joy and a delight to us and would prepare the people for the Lord. It was truly incredible. A miracle. I know that God is faithful. I know this. And yet, I doubted. I doubted that we were chosen.

Reporter: What was your response?

Zechariah: I asked Gabriel how I could be sure because, you know, we were already so old—as if God didn't know that. I know now that it was a ridiculous question.

Reporter: I imagine most people can sympathize, given the circumstances.

Zechariah: Thanks, but they shouldn't. I asked an archangel sent by God how I could be sure of what he was telling me. What was I thinking? How could I not fall on my face and praise God right then and there? I deserved what came next.

Reporter: Not being able to speak?

Zechariah: Yes. Because of my disastrous unbelief, I couldn't talk again until after my son was born. When I

was finally able to, I immediately began praising God—
what I should've done in the first place.

Reporter: What would you like to tell others, in
light of this experience?

Zechariah: Simple. Repent and believe. God
chose you, and He wants to use you, even if you think
it's too late or impossible. Let God be God. Trust Him
and believe.

You are chosen.

PRAYER FOCUS

Acknowledge to God an area in your life you've hardened
your heart about and resolve to be surrendered and
open to anything He wants to do.

MOVING FORWARD

o What is something you've repeatedly petitioned God for?

o Do you struggle to believe God hears
   your prayers?

o What are some audacious things you
   can ask God to do in your life?

HOPE

And we boast in the hope of the glory of God. Not only so, but we also glory in our sufferings, because we know that suffering produces perseverance; perseverance, character; and character, hope. And hope does not put us to shame, because God's love has been poured out into our hearts through the Holy Spirit, who has been given to us.

ROMANS 5:2–5 NIV

Reporter: Elizabeth, tell me what was going through your mind when Zechariah returned from the temple and tried to relay Gabriel's news.

Elizabeth: Well, needless to say, I was shocked that he was unable to speak. Something major had obviously happened, but I had no idea what … or why he couldn't tell me. So I ran to get the writing tablet.

Reporter: And once you read it?

Elizabeth: Oh my! Tears of joy streamed down my cheeks. How could this be? I was in total awe of God's goodness and His favor on us.

Reporter: Your husband asked Gabriel the same question, except not exactly from a place of wonder and awe. Were you disappointed by Zechariah's initial disbelief?

Elizabeth: Zechariah is a good man, a righteous man, but I know how hope deferred can make the heart sick. I was disappointed for him, not in him.

Reporter: You still had hope?

Elizabeth: My desire was for a child, but my hope has always been in the Lord. You know, I think of all the times Zechariah and I prayed for a child during all those years of suffering barrenness, not knowing that every detail of John's conception, birth, and life had already been planned.

Reporter: How did you respond to the news that your child would grow up to be the messenger who, in the strength of Elijah, would herald the arrival of the Messiah?

Elizabeth: I still marvel at how we used to read about "the one calling out in the wilderness," years before we knew that one would be our son. I dropped to my knees in awe of the Lord's favor. I was so completely overwhelmed with joy and gratitude. For the first five months of my pregnancy, I remained in seclusion, relishing the miracle inside me … and what it would mean for God's people. He chose me for this. He chose *me*.

Reporter: Why do you think it all happened the way it did?

Elizabeth: Clearly, John's life was fashioned to fulfill the promises God made through His holy prophets. But why me? Why did I get to be his mother? Only God knows. I imagine He wanted to make it extra clear that it was *all Him*. That nothing is impossible with God. Our miraculous little family is proof. And since no one can deny that, we'll boast all the more in the hope of the glory of God.

We were chosen.

PRAYER FOCUS

Be brave and ask God not to relieve you of the tough circumstances or long wait for answers but to change you through them.

MOVING FORWARD

o What suffering have you experienced that has produced perseverance, character, and hope?

o What was the evidence of your spiritual growth?

o Have you ever been brought to tears over God's goodness and favor? Describe the circumstances.

RESET

John answered them, "I baptize with water,
but among you stands one you do not know,
even he who comes after me, the strap
of whose sandal I am not worthy to untie."

JOHN 1:26–27

John the Baptist was a piece of work. He preached outside the city, heralding the coming Messiah whom the Jews had been eagerly awaiting. Everything about him screamed *wilderness*. Unkempt and ill-mannered, he wore camel's hair and ate bugs, chastising the crowds for their sin no matter their station. Tax collectors, soldiers, and religious leaders alike—no one was spared his message of repentance. But despite his antagonism and poor fashion sense, the people turned out en masse, following him into the literal wilderness to be baptized.

The Israelites were, in fact, very familiar with wilderness living; their history was rich with it. Noah and his family were the only ones spared from the flood of total destruction, so when they stepped off the boat, they stepped into the wilderness of a new world (Genesis 8:15–17). God told Abraham to leave everything behind and follow Him into the wilderness to the home He would show him (12:1). Moses led the Israelites out of slavery in Egypt and into the wilderness where they would walk for forty years before reaching the promised land (Exodus 13:17–22).

And each time the wilderness served as a reset button that says: *Life as you know it is over, and a new thing has begun.*

John's message from the wilderness was clear: *Repent because the Savior of the world is already among you.* What an ominous and cool thing to say, and I imagine it accomplished its intended dramatic effect. No doubt the eyes of the people were wide with wonder when they asked, "Who the heck *are* you? The Messiah? Elijah? Some other super important person we should be excited about?" But John was just the guy pressing the wilderness reset button, and he made sure the people knew it.

I'm not the Messiah, so much so that I'm not even worthy to touch His shoe.

It wouldn't be long before Jesus emerged from

among the crowd, preaching a gospel radically different from what they expected, calling people to leave everything behind and follow Him on the path He would show them, rescuing them from slavery to sin, and by faith granting access to the promised land of heaven. And while He didn't bring an end to the Roman occupation the way they'd assumed the Messiah would, He did indeed make straight the path in the wilderness.

And upon His arrival, the new thing had begun.

PRAYER FOCUS

Ask God to reveal where you might need a reset, then express your willingness to go to the wilderness if necessary.

MOVING FORWARD

o Describe a time in your life when you experienced the wilderness. How did God meet you there?

o How do the words "from among you" impact the way you see Jesus?

o What new thing is God doing in your life and heart right now?

TESTED

He is the image of the invisible God, the firstborn of all creation. For by him all things were created, in heaven and on earth, visible and invisible, whether thrones or dominions or rulers or authorities—all things were created through him and for him. And he is before all things, and in him all things hold together.

COLOSSIANS 1:15–17

All things were created through Jesus. And the factors composing His test in the wilderness were no exception. Matthew 4:1 sets the scene: "Then Jesus was led up by the Spirit into the wilderness to be tempted by the devil." Right off the bat, we're clued into who's in control.

"Then" connotes time. Obviously, so do forty days and nights. Thousands of years before He was miraculously conceived into it, Jesus created the passage of time. Prior to His incarnation, He transcended every physical law and dimension that governs this world; then Jesus set omnipresence aside and surrendered Himself to the vassalage of time.

In the beginning, Jesus created the Judean wilderness. He spoke into existence the rocky terrain, deep ravines, barren grades, and scant vegetation. When He marked out the foundations of the earth, the precise coordinates for this period of His own suffering were noted. Jesus set opulence aside and surrendered Himself to the blistering, desolate landscape.

The body Jesus inhabited was made. He designed His own human suit. He constructed its cellular respiration, metabolic reactions, and biochemical energy, knowing how each of these complex systems would respond to His voluntary deprivation. Jesus was experiencing physiologically what He'd designed supernaturally. He set heavenly perfection aside and surrendered Himself to physical depletion.

Even His tempter was created. God created satan as Lucifer, the highest-ranking angel, who rebelled and was cast to earth, where he has operated as the devil ever since. How satan became evil is unexplained; God saw fit to keep that part a mystery. But what the testing in the wilderness makes crystal clear is that nothing can foil God's divine purposes, not timing, not harrowing circumstances, and certainly not satan. For the sake of our being chosen, Jesus put all opposition in its place, literally. Then He was led by the Spirit to surrender Himself to the will of the Father.

The disciples were tested, the religious leaders were tested, Pilate was tested, we are tested. We can't know in advance how we'll respond to it, and success or failure is not determined by us. But make no mistake—the test is not an accident.

PRAYER FOCUS

No one likes tests. Ask God to help you not only survive them but to thrive under them and to be drawn closer to Him through them.

MOVING FORWARD

o Do you believe God has designed all the elements composing your tests? Explain why or why not.

o What's the most difficult test you've ever had to surrender to?

o Whether you're in a test now or one is coming, what are some ways you can better withstand it?

PROCLAIM

"The Spirit of the Lord is upon me, because he has
anointed me to proclaim good news to the poor.
He has sent me to proclaim liberty to the captives
and recovering of sight to the blind, to set at liberty
those who are oppressed, to proclaim the year
of the Lord's favor."

LUKE 4:18–19

Many people have said Jesus never claimed to be God—
that He was a good man and a powerful teacher, a
humanitarian and an example we should follow, but that
He didn't actually claim to be more than that and His
followers added the "divine" part.

Incorrect.

Take for instance this moment in the synagogue
in Nazareth, His hometown. He showed up on a Sabbath

day like He'd always done and volunteered to read from the scroll of the prophet Isaiah. He found the place where our verse of the day was written (a verse written in the eighth century BC about the coming Messiah) and read it out loud. Then He sat down and said, "Today this Scripture has been fulfilled in your hearing" (v. 21).

Um, excuse me?

How crazy that statement must've seemed to the people who'd attended a gazillion Shabbat services with Jesus. He'd grown up in their small town, sat under the rabbis' teaching, played games with kids in the street, whittled wood with His dad, and—according to the Bible—wasn't above average in any visible way.

And during Jesus' life of thirty years (not to mention the four hundred prior), the people were eagerly waiting for the Messiah—the one who would be king and liberate them from oppressive Roman rule. At least, that's what they assumed the Messiah would be and do. But they misunderstood the prophecies.

To proclaim good news to the poor.

Jesus came preaching heaven, its riches, its beauty, its infinity, and its availability. He came with the message that there's more to life than what we see— more for those literally disenfranchised and more for those impoverished in their souls.

To proclaim liberty to the captives.

Jesus wasn't a political liberator; He was a spiritual

liberator. He came to pronounce freedom from the sin that enslaves and all the eternal consequences it ensures.

Recovering of sight to the blind.

Jesus healed people physically, but the physical healing was only a picture of what was necessary spiritually. Jesus came to open people's eyes and hearts to their sin, to their need for help and mercy, and to His desire and ability to restore them.

To proclaim the year of the Lord's favor.

Jesus and the gift of salvation He would offer expressed God's favor toward us, a world in desperate need of Him.

Jesus was indeed a good man and a powerful teacher, one who was kind and loving and inclusive and all that. But He also claimed to be the fulfillment of Old Testament prophecy regarding the one who would save the world. And on that Sabbath day in His quiet hometown, He proclaimed it in a way *no one* in the room misunderstood.

The long-foretold Messiah you've been preaching about in your synagogues for centuries?

I'm Him.

PRAYER FOCUS

Thank God for His heart for the oppressed, ask Him to give you that same heart, and then ask Him for courage to proclaim the good news as boldly as Jesus did.

MOVING FORWARD

o Which of Jesus' character qualities most stand out to you in this story?

o Why do you think Jesus began His three years of ministry with this particular public display in His hometown?

o What are ways you can display the same love for those Jesus came for as the prophecies indicate?

REJECTED

And he said, "Truly, I say to you, no prophet is acceptable in his hometown …" When they heard these things, all in the synagogue were filled with wrath. And they rose up and drove him out of the town and brought him to the brow of the hill on which their town was built, so that they could throw him down the cliff. But passing through their midst, he went away.

LUKE 4:24, 28–30

As the saying goes, familiarity breeds contempt. Which means when Jesus went home for a visit, it didn't go so great. He attended synagogue and volunteered to read. When He sat back down and said, "Today this Scripture has been fulfilled in your hearing" (Luke 4:21), they seemed cool with it. Jesus was being gracious enough— odd but gracious, so they "spoke well of him" (v. 22).

But then Jesus didn't return the favor. Knowing their hearts, He responded with, "No prophet is accepted in his hometown" (v. 24 NIV). It was a dig. He followed up with a reminder that Elijah and Elisha weren't sent to heal their own people, because it would've been a waste of time.

Uffdah. Jesus effectively told His hometown crowd they had the same issue as their Old Testament relatives—and they came unglued. So much so, they wanted Him dead. With scant provocation from the guy they'd known for thirty years, the Nazarenes became so insanely offended and incensed that they drove Jesus out of town and up a hill so they could throw Him off a cliff. They were going to murder Mary and Joseph's boy.

Extreme? Yes. Expected? You bet. That day Jesus had read from the prophet Isaiah, who proclaimed the coming Messiah along with the response the Messiah's presence would engender from humankind: He would be "despised and rejected" (Isaiah 53:3).

Sad.

These people knew Jesus. They should've been all the more in awe of God's power and authority clearly on display in Him. What the heck else could it be? He was the carpenter who grew up with them, and now He was preaching and healing all over the place. But we tend to reject anything or anyone that represents a big change in understanding or perspective, even if it comes from someone familiar—*especially* from someone familiar. The notion that what they thought they knew could be wrong was as incomprehensible as the notion of changing your mind in a Facebook argument. So they hardened their hearts, hated Him, and tried to push Him off a cliff.

In doing so, they fulfilled Old Testament prophecy: "He was despised and rejected by mankind, a man of suffering, and familiar with pain. Like one from whom people hide their faces he was despised, and we held him in low esteem" (Isaiah 53:3 NIV). Oh, the irony.

PRAYER FOCUS

Ask God to give you the humility necessary to hear truth when it's spoken, as well as the wisdom and clarity to know how to respond.

MOVING FORWARD

o Are you more likely to accept advice or godly counsel from a close friend or a mere acquaintance? Why or why not?

o What caused people to despise and reject Jesus? What was it that caused you to reject Him prior to your salvation?

o When was the last time you changed your perspective or realized you were wrong about something significant? (Note: if it's hard to remember, that might be something to work on.)

AUTHORITY

And [Jesus] went down to Capernaum, a city of
Galilee. And he was teaching them on the Sabbath,
and they were astonished at his teaching, for his
words possessed authority.

LUKE 4:31–32

In Jesus' day, authority was limited to a select few. The
Jews had a religious system that not only governed their
places of worship; it also determined the laws of the
land politically, culturally, and socially. Religious leaders
had authority to tell everyone else how to live because
they were the ruling class of Israel. As high priests
tasked with interpreting the law of Moses, they also
determined what constituted crimes and often carried
out punishments, sometimes in the middle of the street.
No trial or appeal to a higher court was given because

they ran the show. So you can imagine how off-putting it was when a carpenter's son turned their well-oiled governing machine on its ear—and the people loved Him to boot.

Stepping into such a rigid system, it wouldn't take long for Jesus to make a name for Himself. "When the sun was setting, all those … with various diseases [were] brought to him, and he laid his hands on every one of them and healed them" (Luke 4:40). No doubt the healing thing drew crowds of people to Jesus, but the Bible repeatedly says they were also in awe of the authoritative way He spoke, and that people came from far and wide to hear Him.

What must a person sound like to solicit awe? "He speaks with authority" is such a specific observation, yet people made it repeatedly. And spoiler alert, the way He spoke is what got Him killed. The religious rulers were terrified of losing their power, and only someone with authority greater than their own could threaten it.

Luke 20:1–2 records one such confrontation: "One day, as Jesus was teaching the people in the temple and preaching the gospel, the chief priests and the scribes with the elders came up and said to him, 'Tell us by what authority you do these things, or who it is that gave you this authority.'"

The Jews tried to understand where the authority that oozed out of Jesus came from. *Who granted it? Who taught you how to speak this way? What entitles you to come onto our turf and teach our people?*

His answer was simple but would seal His fate: "Truly, truly, I say to you, before Abraham was, I am" (John 8:58).

And there it was. The claim that made both the way Jesus spoke and the reaction He received make sense. "I AM" was the name God gave Himself when He sent Moses to free the Israelites from Egypt (Exodus 3), and the way He continually referred to Himself in the book of Isaiah—and His listeners were well versed in the Scripture He referenced.

Simply put, Jesus spoke by His *own* authority.

Of course, He was never at a loss for how to respond to questions or how to interpret the Law—He wrote it. Of course, He didn't fear the Romans or any other governing body—empires rose and fell by His word. The authority with which He spoke was His own. He is the one who whispered the world into existence; who holds planets in orbit and mountains in their place; who commands tides to rise and orchards to bloom; who created things like E minor and puppies; who rose from the dead—and we'll all give account to Him one day.

So yeah, His preaching was worth the trip.

PRAYER FOCUS

Thank God that He's in control and you're not, repent of areas of your life that aren't under His authority, and ask Him for help in submitting.

MOVING FORWARD

o Is there an area in your life where you're denying Christ's authority?

o In what ways does His authority bring peace and comfort to your circumstances?

o What's your plan for how to submit more fully to Christ's authority?

BOLDNESS

"So I say to you: Ask and it will be given to you;
seek and you will find; knock and the door
will be opened to you."

Luke 11:9 NIV

Andrew was an early adopter of the ask, seek, and knock principle. As far as we know, Andrew was the first of the twelve disciples to ask Jesus for anything.

It started the moment they met, which happened to be right after John the Baptist pointed Jesus out. Andrew was a disciple of John's, so when the guy who'd been preparing the way for the Lamb of God shouted, "Behold, the Lamb of God" (John 1:29), Andrew didn't waste any time. He and another of John the Baptist's disciples took off after Jesus.

"What do you want?" Jesus asked.

They answered with a question: "Where are you staying?" (v. 38 NIV).

Jesus rewarded their boldness with an invitation to spend the day with Him, so they followed Him to His place—where Jesus opened the door. In other words, one proverbial knock led to one actual conversation, and they knew they'd found the Messiah.

Andrew ran and told his brother Simon. And when Jesus called Simon on a beach, Simon and Andrew dropped everything and ran to follow Him. It was a whirlwind, game-changer of a day that all started with the simple question: *What do you want?*

They wanted Jesus.

When the ministry was in full swing, a disciple asked Jesus to teach them to pray the way John the Baptist taught his disciples (Luke 11:1). It's not a stretch to assume it was Andrew, the former John the Baptist follower who wasn't shy about asking Jesus for stuff. Jesus again obliged and taught them the Lord's Prayer, then continued with a story about an audacious asker—a guy who knocked on a friend's door at midnight wanting three loaves of bread. The friend was in bed and the house was locked, but he got up anyway—not because his friend was asking, Jesus explained, but because of the guy's crazy midnight-asking boldness. Jesus punctuated the story with the famous exhortation: "Ask and it will be given to you; seek and you will find; knock and the door will be opened to you" (v. 9 NIV).

Jesus and Andrew's initial exchange is a sweet and simple proof of the "seek and find" promise. Andrew was bold. He wanted answers, so he asked. He sought after the Messiah, and Jesus opened His door to him and gave him the Bread of Life.

Jesus asks us the exact same question: *What do you want?*

You never know, the answer could incite a whirlwind game-changer of a day.

PRAYER FOCUS

Be bold. Ask God for wisdom and growth and life change, then ask Him for clarity in areas of life you're confused about.

MOVING FORWARD

o   Describe a time you felt bold in approaching Jesus. What did you ask for?

o   How did He answer you?

o   How would you answer Jesus' question: *What do you want?*

ROCK

"And I tell you, you are Peter, and on this rock I will build my church, and the gates of hell shall not prevail against it. I will give you the keys of the kingdom of heaven, and whatever you bind on earth shall be bound in heaven, and whatever you loose on earth shall be loosed in heaven."

MATTHEW 16:18–19

His name was Simon. So what a strange and presumptuous "how do you do?" to be told your new name would be Peter. (*I'm sorry—what?*) His brother, Andrew, was all in already. He'd been a disciple of John the Baptist, and when John identified Jesus as the Messiah, it was all the proof Andrew needed. He became one of Jesus' first disciples, and he was good at it. By all accounts, Andrew was steady, studied, good-natured, and easy to have around. As for Simon? Not so much.

Simon Peter was emotional. When Jesus tried to wash his feet, Peter refused to allow the Master's humbling act of service: "[But] Jesus answered him, 'If I do not wash you, you have no share with me.' [So] Simon Peter said to him, 'Lord, not my feet only but also my hands and my head!'" (John 13:8–9). As it often did, the feelings pendulum swung.

Simon Peter was impulsive. When soldiers came to arrest Jesus, Peter drew his sword and cut off a guy's ear (18:10). It was perhaps the most ineffective countermeasure possible to take on an entire temple guard by way of one man's ear. Not sure what the plan was there.

Sometimes Simon Peter was afraid of stuff. After Jesus' arrest, all of Peter's ear-cutting bravado vanished. To avoid being arrested, he denied even knowing Jesus—not once but three times, just as Christ predicted he would (vv. 17, 25–27).

All of his instability begs the question, Why did Jesus call him Peter? Especially considering the name Peter means "rock."

The answer? Jesus makes us what we're not.

Notice some correlations between pre-Jesus Peter and post-Jesus Peter:

o   Pre-Jesus Peter was directed by

emotion. Post-Jesus Peter was directed by his intense love for Jesus.

o Pre-Jesus Peter was impulsive. Post-Jesus Peter was stable, but the culture was not. Christianity was changing everything, and leading that charge required the ability to adjust, pivot, and respond to the Holy Spirit on the fly.

o Pre-Jesus Peter was afraid. Post-Jesus Peter was afraid of ever turning his back on Jesus again, therefore becoming fearless regarding everything else.

And the same power that transformed the unruly fisherman is at work in all who believe. Jesus accepts us as we are, but He knows who we'll become by His power, and He's making us what we're not yet.

PRAYER FOCUS

Ask God to reveal a sinful part of you that you think is "just the way I am," and ask Him to make you something you're not.

MOVING FORWARD

o What are your primary weaknesses?

o In what ways have you seen God trans-form your heart and mind?

o Write down a weakness you want to turn into a strength and commit to praying for help and working on it.

REPENT

After John was put in prison, Jesus went into Galilee,
proclaiming the good news of God, "The time has
come," he said. "The kingdom of God has come near.
Repent and believe the good news!"

MARK 1:14–15 NIV

Despite popular consensus, teaching folks to "love
thy neighbor" was not Jesus' main thing. Nor was
it convincing them to turn the other cheek, to be
hospitable, or to help the poor. All good things, just not
the main thing.

This was the main thing: Jesus came to proclaim
the kingdom of heaven—God's sovereign rule and reign,
now and for all of eternity.

How did He go about it? By picking up where
His predecessor left off. Like John the Baptist, Jesus

commanded all who would listen to repent and believe. Following more rules wasn't part of the equation, lest someone think salvation could be earned.

Jesus was calling for heart change. Radical inward transformation was the price of kingdom admission. Nothing more. Nothing less. And it just so happened that a disastrous night of fishing, followed by a boatload of revelation (pun intended) set the stage for Simon to experience just that.

Knowing Simon had an unsuccessful night of fishing, Jesus told him to go back out into the deep and let down the nets (Luke 5:4–5). Peter complied.

As soon as the nets hit the water, they were filled beyond capacity. So much so, Simon and Andrew needed help from others to handle it. Very quickly, both boats were nearly sinking with the massive haul of fish.

That's what did it. The miraculous catch compelled Simon to fall to his knees in front of Jesus and say, "Go away from me, Lord; I am a sinful man!" (v. 8 NIV). Because that's what miracles do—they bear witness to the sovereignty of God and expose human frailty. Which should result in what Simon did: repentance.

"Do not be afraid," Jesus responded. "From now on you will fish for people" (v. 10 NIV). And just like that, Simon went from being questioning to sure. He and the men pulled their boats out of the water, left everything, and followed Jesus.

It wouldn't be the last time Simon would come face-to-face with his weaknesses; it was a reoccurring theme. So was repentance. So was forgiveness, which was why Jesus would repeatedly send Simon back into the deep. There were more men to catch and hearts in need of changing. But because of his own repentant heart, Simon would pick up where his predecessor left off and proclaim the kingdom of heaven—God's sovereign rule and reign, now and for all of eternity.

PRAYER FOCUS

Pray to God for repentance for as many things as you can think of, but end the prayer with gratitude for His forgiveness.

MOVING FORWARD

o What do you focus on more: Jesus' command to love others ... or to repent and believe?

o What incident in your life incited radical inward transformation? Would you regard it as a miracle?

o Repentance fosters humility and surrender, so what can you repent of?

COME AND SEE

The next day Jesus decided to go to Galilee. He found
Philip and said to him, "Follow me." … Philip found
Nathanael and said to him, "We have found him of
whom Moses in the Law and also the prophets wrote,
Jesus of Nazareth, the son of Joseph. Nathanael said
to him, "Can anything good come out of Nazareth?"
Philip said to him, "Come and see."

JOHN 1:43, 45–46

Come and see—what an interesting strategy. Like
Andrew and Peter, Philip hardly knew the one he
now believed was the Messiah. In fact, the only thing
we know for sure is that Jesus said, "Follow me," and
suddenly Philip was proselytizing in His name.

But why? What occurred between the seeing and

the following? Nathanael's first few moments with Jesus give us a clue.

> Jesus saw Nathanael coming toward him and said of him, "Behold, an Israelite in whom there is no deceit!" Nathanael said to him, "How do you know me?" Jesus answered him, "Before Philip called you, when you were under the fig tree, I saw you." Nathanael answered him, "Rabbi, you are the Son of God! You are the King of Israel!" (John 1:47–49)

Jesus had a disarming way about Him. Nathanael was humoring his friend Philip and probably his own curiosity, but he was skeptical of Jesus and clearly a bit prejudiced. The town of Nazareth was very small and considered by its neighbors to be uneducated, unreformed, and unrefined. So in Nathanael's mind, anyone born and raised there couldn't possibly be the Messiah they'd been waiting for—and he was quick to say so. Which made Jesus' first words to him so interesting and gracious. Instead of, "Behold, an Israelite in whom there is bigotry and zero tact," Jesus called him honest and took Nathanael off guard. He was indeed a person who spoke his mind, and he was proud of it. He was practical and learned and dealt in brass tacks—but how did the Nazarene know that?

Because Jesus had been watching him, and not just while he sat under a tree. The one-two punch of knowing Nathanael's whereabouts along with the values that made him tick (unredeemed though they were), was evidence of the supernatural that set Jesus apart. And so Philip's come-and-see strategy proved effective because Jesus did the convincing.

As He always does.

> Jesus answered him, "Because I said to you, 'I saw you under a fig tree,' you believe? You will see greater things than these … Truly, truly, I say to you, you will see heaven opened, and the angels of God ascending and descending on the Son of Man." (John 1:50–51)

I imagine Nathanael's 180 made Jesus chuckle. No doubt there was an omniscient smirk on His face, knowing the signs and wonders Nathanael would come to see on a daily basis—and for the rest of his life.

But sure, the fig tree thing was cool.

PRAYER FOCUS

Thank God that He allowed you to "come and see," and ask Him for direction: *Who can I introduce to Jesus and how?*

MOVING FORWARD

o Write out your come-to-Jesus story. How did you meet Him? How did He change your mind about who He is and what's true?

o Since Jesus is no longer walking and talking on earth, what does "come and see" mean now?

o Who is someone in your life who needs to "come and see" Jesus? Pray for that person, then go make the introduction. Trust Jesus to do the convincing.

EMMANUEL

Now there were six stone water jars there for the Jewish rites of purification, each holding twenty or thirty gallons. Jesus said to the servants, "Fill the jars with water." And they filled them up to the brim. And he said to them, "Now draw some out and take it to the master of the feast." So they took it. When the master of the feast tasted the water now become wine, and did not know where it came from (though the servants who had drawn the water knew), the master of the feast called the bridegroom and said to him, "Everyone serves the good wine first, and when people have drunk freely, then the poor wine. But you have kept the good wine until now." This, the first of his signs, Jesus did at Cana in Galilee, and manifested his glory. And his disciples believed in him.

JOHN 2:6–11

There was a bona fide crisis underway. Back in Jesus' day, wine was a staple at most meals and a must at any respectable celebration. But at this wedding, the wine had run out—a humiliation of epic proportions for the groom's family, who was hosting the party. Jesus' mother, Mary, took it upon herself to find Jesus and bring Him up to speed.

"They have no wine," were her words (John 2:3), but her sense of urgency and meaning were clear—*Help!* No one in attendance except His mother had reason to believe Jesus could provide; He was as poor as anyone. He was seemingly normal. Up until that moment, there was little to set Him apart from the other partygoers, which makes His mother-directed debut a precious backdrop to what followed (vv. 5–11).

Jesus' newly recruited disciples watched as He instructed the servants to fill giant jars with water. What a confusing but intriguing directive. The servants did as they were told, which included taking a glass of water to their superior, the master of the feast, who apparently knew nothing of the looming drama. And then at some point between the drawing and the giving, the water turned into wine. Not just any wine but awesome wine, the quality of which brought honor to the host since common practice was to serve the cheap stuff as soon as guests were too drunk to notice. The party and reputation of his friends were saved, but of all the miracles Jesus could've performed first, He chose a wedding and wine and only a few witnesses.

Why?

Because He's Emmanuel—"God with us" (Matthew 1:23).

The setting of His first miracle, the need in front of Jesus (potential embarrassment), and His obedience to His mom were consistent with everything else in His life: He was ordinary. Jesus was born in a stable, raised by simple people, and worked as a carpenter like His dad. He attended school and synagogue—and now a party—because God's method of rescuing the world was to enter into it.

For the next three years, the disciples saw Jesus do extraordinary things in ordinary, everyday circumstances. They watched the Messiah be hungry, happy, tired, frustrated, angry, and—in the garden of Gethsemane—afraid. They saw Him love on the poor and rich alike, often using the common to display His heavenly glory, like loaves and fish, mud, waves, trees, and tombs. They learned to minister to real people with real problems, to love without prejudice, to preach the gospel no matter the conditions, to perform miracles, and to obey unto death.

And through it all, the disciples followed in His steps because of their faith in the one who was with them: Emmanuel—God with us, who "dwelt among us, and we have seen his glory, glory as of the only Son from the Father, full of grace and truth" (John 1:14).

PRAYER FOCUS

Thank God for "Emmanuel" and ask Him for help in your pursuit to find the extraordinary in your ordinary.

MOVING FORWARD

- o At this moment, what circumstances are most difficult for you?

- o How should knowing that God is with you affect the way you respond to your circumstances?

- o Just as the servants at the wedding had to draw water before they actually saw the water turn into wine, what are ways you can step out in faith as a result of His promise to be with you?

WORRY

"But seek first his kingdom and his righteousness, and all these things will be given to you as well. Therefore, do not worry about tomorrow, for tomorrow will worry about itself. Each day has enough trouble of its own."

MATTHEW 6:33–34 NIV

Trouble. Each day has plenty of it, and tomorrow will usher in more. That part of the teaching the disciples had no problem accepting. It was the "do not worry" part that proved trickier. In fact, the entirety of their ministry would be spent trying to understand Jesus' triumph over every kind of trouble.

Jesus could've kicked off His signs and wonders with a parting-of-the-Red-Sea-caliber miracle. Instead, He chose a simpler approach—He changed water into wine because it ran out. It was a relatively minor problem Jesus was asked to solve. His mother was anxious on behalf of the wedding hosts and wanted Him to step in—so He did. Which means it was during a party that Jesus chose to reveal His glory to His disciples for the first time. It was the public debut of triumph over trouble.

In doing so, Jesus demonstrated that nothing is inconsequential. Every predicament is an opportunity for divine intervention and continued celebration.

We too tend to worry about issues large and small, and Jesus cares about each one, especially because of the opportunity they present—but we have to do our part. Like Mary, we have to ask even with seemingly small matters. Otherwise, we'll read verses about not worrying and worry even more about our inability to cease worrying, rather than seeking and asking so that Jesus can prove Himself triumphant.

Perhaps that's why He honored His mother's request. The simplicity of it represents so many kingdom principles. For example, it takes faith to surrender our worries and trade them in for kingdom seeking and Jesus trusting. When we do, He goes to work on our behalf. Of course, that doesn't mean He's literally going to turn water into wine, but He's going to always do the spiritual equivalent: work things out for good for those who love Him (Romans 8:28).

Trust Him with the little things, and He'll prove

time and again that you can trust Him with everything. And don't worry about whether or not you have the ability to cease worrying. You don't. That's the point. Your job is to seek Jesus and His righteousness. His response will be to reveal more of His glory, and the outcome will be your refreshed and increased faith. And, miraculously, a whole lot less worrying.

PRAYER FOCUS

Ask God to right-size your fears and expectations so that you can see struggles as He sees them—opportunities.

MOVING FORWARD

o Do you struggle with anxiety? What things do you tend to worry about the most and why?

o Jesus used an everyday occasion to reveal His glory. Describe a common event in your life through which He revealed His glory and increased your faith.

o Do you ask for Jesus' help with the seemingly small stuff? Why or why not?

TRUST

Trust in the LORD with all your heart and lean not on your own understanding; in all your ways submit to him, and he will make your paths straight.

PROVERBS 3:5–6 NIV

Matthew was an easy guy to hate because he was a money-grubbing tax collector. On behalf of the Roman Empire, he and his comrades extorted their fellow Jews far beyond what was owed to the government.

And Matthew was perfectly cool with that.

The corrupt system worked in his favor. It was a great gig since Matthew was all about Matthew and excelled at doing exactly what Solomon warned against in Proverbs 23:4: "Do not toil to acquire wealth; be discerning enough to desist." On the contrary, Matthew was wearing himself out to get rich. He was trusting in his cleverness.

Pre-Jesus Matthew's response would've been, *So what, man? If you're going to wear yourself out doing something, it might as well be getting rich. Besides, if you can't trust yourself, who in the world can you trust?*

We get it, Pre-Jesus Matthew. We get it.

Because, sadly, that's exactly the kind of self-reliant, succeed-at-all-costs, follow-your-own-truth ethos our world goes bananas over. Our culture of consumerism feasts on it. I mean, who doesn't love a good rags-to-riches story? And if those riches were attained through disgustingly selfish, ill-gotten, greedy means ... Eh. Details.

The desire to be on top is like an electromagnetic force. And it can seize any one of us, like a thumbtack sucked up by a magnet. So then, think about what it would take to reverse that mighty pull once you'd been seized. What would cause you to willingly give it up, walk away from the money, and lay down the power?

Only the most dramatic of plot twists. For Matthew, it came in the form of two simple yet profound words: "Follow me." Jesus "went out and saw a tax collector ... sitting at the tax booth. And he said to him, 'Follow me.' And leaving everything, he rose and followed him" (Luke 5:27–28).

This was not a casual interaction. In a single

moment, Matthew's need for more stuff was obliterated when he stood face-to-face with the Author of Life. All the trust-in-yourself and follow-your-own-truth nonsense vaporized the second he locked eyes with Truth and was called to follow the ultimate force, the desire to know and love God in the flesh. Matthew, the easy-to-hate, crooked, money-grubbing tax collector was standing in the presence of pure love. And it changed him instantly. Radically.

We get it, Matthew. We get it!

Because, beautifully, that's exactly the kind of Jesus-reliant, trust-at-all-costs, "follow me" ethos our heavenly Father goes bananas over. So much so, He orchestrates a plot twist for each of us to respond to. And we too must decide. God longs to make our crooked paths straight (Luke 3:5) and script the ultimate rags-to-riches story, which sometimes involves trading in our earthly riches for a few temporary rags.

And Matthew was perfectly cool with that.

He saw how much more this redemptive system worked in his favor. It was a great gig, as Matthew became all about Jesus.

PRAYER FOCUS

Thank God for asking you to follow Him, repent of the times you rely on your own skills, and ask Him to show you areas where you can shift your allegiances.

MOVING FORWARD

o In what areas of your life do you trust in your own cleverness?

o If you're brutally honest, do you identify more with pre-Jesus Matthew or disciple Matthew?

o What have been some of the dramatic plot twists the Lord has orchestrated in your life?

USEFUL

Therefore, if anyone cleanses himself from these things, he will be a vessel for honor, sanctified, useful to the Master, prepared for every good work.

2 Timothy 2:21 NASB

A vessel (think water pitcher) is designed and created for the purpose of containing something. A utensil (think fork or knife) is designed and created for the purpose of doing something.

And "those who cleanse themselves" become vessels (2 Timothy 2:21 NIV).

As Christ followers, there are plenty of things we're exhorted to do. Yet we are never referred to as ordinary utensils; rather, we are chosen instruments—vessels. Ergo, we are to contain more than do.

Of course, this begs the question, *What are we*

supposed to contain? As obvious as the answer should be, it's just not. Throughout Scripture we're told repeatedly that human beings are vessels designed and created for the purpose of containing … God.

Still, we tend to get hung up on utility. We have this proclivity for assessing people based solely on what they can do.

Take Matthew, for instance, and why he was chosen to be a disciple.

His ability to keep a ledger for the Romans while pilfering a pile of cash for himself demonstrated a keen proficiency in accounting. Check.

He was also literate, a bonus skill that would come in handy for future Gospel writing. Check.

Personality-wise, Matthew wasn't shy about public appearances. Check.

He wasn't timid or apologetic about rendering his tax-collecting services. In fact, that persistent workaholic attitude would prove especially useful when carrying out the Great Commission. Check. Check. Check.

All true. But no, that's human logic.

Jesus didn't see Matthew sitting at his collection booth and think, *Oh, perfect. I don't have an aggressive numbers guy yet.* He wasn't rounding out His team based on their resumes, core competencies, and Myers-Briggs results. In fact, their prior accomplishments were effectively useless, as evidenced by the five thousand folks served fish by the fishermen who had nothing to do with the catch.

Jesus didn't need ability. He required availability.

Matthew was not chosen based on what he could do. He was called because of what he was willing to give up, which was everything. He chose to take Jesus at His word: "Whoever finds their life will lose it, and whoever loses their life for my sake will find it" (Matthew 10:39 NIV).

And Matthew found it. He walked away from all the stuff, handed over the keys, and vacated the premises. He became a vessel of honor, sanctified, useful to the Master, and prepared for every good work. He was ready to go and do, only because of what he contained.

Matthew was a vessel designed and created for the purpose of containing God. And he nailed it.

PRAYER FOCUS

Thank God He doesn't value you for what you do, then ask Him to reveal things you can do for Him that don't necessarily require your natural skills.

MOVING FORWARD

o In what ways do you tend to focus more on what you can do than on the one whose Spirit you contain?

o Can you think of anyone you value more because of what they do than who they are in Christ?

o How can you make yourself more available?

DAY 22

ALL Y'ALL

And the Pharisees and their scribes grumbled at his
disciples, saying, "Why do you eat and drink with tax
collectors and sinners?" And Jesus answered them,
"Those who are well have no need of a physician,
but those who are sick. I have not come to call the
righteous but sinners to repentance."

Luke 5:30–32

To grumble not at *Jesus* but at His disciples—what a
passive-aggressive way for the Pharisees and scribes to
behave. They had the legal authority (and personalities)
to chastise Jesus; instead, they directed their challenge
to the ones they were insulting.

And I imagine this ragtag dinner party had no
idea how to respond. All of it was so new: They just
met Jesus, so while they were thinking He was maybe

the long-awaited Messiah, they couldn't have been 100 percent sure. Not to mention they were, in fact, hanging out with society's most despised—a category that included a few of them. Certainly the Pharisees' question had crossed the minds of everyone sitting at the table.

I'll bet they leaned in to hear Jesus' response.

He had recently gained a lot of notoriety. People were traveling from Galilee, Judea, and Jerusalem to hear Him preach and see Him heal. No doubt the assumption of the religious leaders was that He'd be impressive—that He'd look and behave like them; like someone worthy of the reports they were getting.

On the contrary.

Instead, they found a normal-looking guy, hanging out with normal people, doing normal people things like eating—that is, when He wasn't casting out demons and making blind men see. Luke 5:29 says that Jesus was "reclining at [the] table with them." He was relaxed and shooting the breeze. He was getting to know them (and they Him) when the Pharisees showed up at Matthew's house uninvited.

I wonder if they rang the doorbell before barging in. I wonder if they stood in the corner whispering like middle school girls. I wonder if they grumbled loudly but pretended Jesus couldn't hear them from three feet away. I wonder if they came prepared with specific questions but changed course when they saw Jesus with the riffraff. I wonder if anyone at the table was offended by their question, or if they were too used to being hated and judged to care. I wonder if the Pharisees' question endeared the insulted guests to Jesus all the more.

Surely His answer did.

I'll see your passive-aggressive, indirect question and raise you with an indirect statement of my own—I'm calling sinners to repentance, not the righteous.

Hmm. While His answer shut them up (which was no doubt fun for the spectators), I have a feeling the Pharisees sensed the meaning of Romans 3:10–12: "None is righteous, no, not one; no one understands; no one seeks God. All have turned aside; together they have become worthless; no one does good, no, not one."

Perhaps a more direct response would've been, "I'm hanging out with the people who know they need me. I don't hang out with people who are too self-righteous to know they need me. But you do need me. All y'all desperately do."

PRAYER FOCUS

Thank God for offering health for your sin sickness and ask Him to give you the same soft heart toward the "sick" that Christ had.

MOVING FORWARD

o What are the areas of your life where you need a "physician"?

o When have you been guilty of the Pharisees' judgment here?

o Who do you know who wouldn't be considered "healthy" by church leaders, and how can you treat them as Jesus treated the "sick"?

RELATIONSHIP

Now when he was in Jerusalem at the Passover
Feast, many believed in his name when they saw the
signs that he was doing. But Jesus on his part did not
entrust himself to them, because he knew all people
and needed no one to bear witness about man, for he
himself knew what was in man.

JOHN 2:23–25

From Adam's first breath, God has been watching.
Every choice, every thought, every motive for every
act—can you imagine what He's seen? Sure, there have
been moments of goodness, righteousness, and love;
many were recorded in Scripture and rewarded by God.
But the bad far outweighs the good. Look at today's
headlines and multiply the negative by a gazillion, and

you'll begin to grasp just how wretched and sinful the human race is.

Jesus was doing amazing things in Jerusalem, and the people were in awe. They followed Him around and listened while He preached, no doubt motivated by the things they were seeing. In other words, as long as the people were experiencing miracles, they were willing to stay. But being in attendance, being in awe, being emotionally impacted, and even believing in the supernatural don't always result in a relationship with Jesus.

Case in point:

On the way to Jerusalem he was passing along between Samaria and Galilee. And as he entered a village, he was met by ten lepers, who stood at a distance and lifted up their voices, saying, "Jesus, Master, have mercy on us." When he saw them he said to them, "Go and show yourselves to the priests." And as they went they were cleansed. Then one of them, when he saw that he was healed, turned back, praising God with a loud voice; and he fell on his face at Jesus' feet, giving him thanks. Now he was a Samaritan. Then Jesus answered, "Were not ten cleansed? Where are the nine? Was no one found to return and give praise to God

except this foreigner?" And he said to him,
"Rise and go your way; your faith has made
you well." (Luke 17:11–19)

The lepers called Him Master and begged for
mercy. And Jesus obliged. He sent them to the priests
because according to the Law, lepers had to be deemed
clean in order to reenter society. They obeyed and went,
and along the way were miraculously healed, which
means by the time they arrived at the synagogue, the
priests did indeed pronounce them clean. After that, I'm
guessing most of them ran home to their families and
friends, then resumed their lives.

Only one of the ten ran back to thank Jesus. Why?

Jesus posed the same question, but it was
rhetorical because He knew what was in that man. He'd
been watching since the beginning.

Far too often, people want the perks of a
relationship with Jesus without the actual relationship.
They take credit when things go well and offer up Hail
Mary prayers when things go badly. They attend church,
but only on holidays. They want assurance of heaven
while maintaining devotion to the world. They have a
faith-someday mentality—*I'll go to Jesus when I'm older;
when I'm done living life on my terms*. But unfortunately,
human terms are sin soaked.

Jesus is looking for people who are willing to run

to Him, to fall on their faces, to repent, surrender, and worship because of who He is, and to learn and grow in a faith that remains even when the miracles cease. Jesus knew what was in people's hearts—it's the reason He came. And so, true believers aren't just in it for the miracles; they have been fundamentally and irrevocably changed by Jesus Himself, making relationship with Him the ultimate prize.

PRAYER FOCUS

Thank God for the relationship He offers and ask Him to not leave you alone so you can be closer to Him as often as possible.

MOVING FORWARD

o Can you think of a time your relationship with Jesus lagged? Is it now?

o What miraculous changes has Jesus made in your heart since you started following Him?

o Moving forward, how can you embrace heart changes over physical ones?

CLEAN

While he was in one of the cities,
there came a man full of leprosy.
And when he saw Jesus,
he fell on his face and begged him,
"Lord, if you will, you can make me clean."

LUKE 5:12

In Christ's time, leprosy was a vicious condition with no known cure. It caused lumps as well as scalelike wounds to grow all over a person's body and could lead to the complete degeneration of the skin and twisting of the bones, ultimately deforming its victims. Fingers, toes, ears, and noses would rot away and fall off, making it difficult for a person to breathe and more likely for them to go blind, as well as making it impossible to do the daily work required to survive.

Those suspected of contracting the disease had to show themselves to the priest, who would evaluate their condition, diagnosing them as clean or unclean. And "unclean" meant you were counted as good as dead and banished from the city to keep the disease from spreading. Lepers were forced to live in tents or caves in designated colonies in the wilderness, wore bells in order to alert people to their presence, and were required to yell, "Unclean! Unclean!" should anyone accidentally come within the legal range.

Having been ripped from their homes, families, friends, and all other comforts in life, the only hope of relief for them was death.

Enter Jesus.

News of the preaching healer had been spreading from town to town—to leper colony. Luke says there was a man "full of leprosy" who approached Jesus, which means (1) he'd had the disease for a while, (2) he'd been living in physical and emotional hell, and (3) somehow there remained in him a modicum of hope enough to violate the law and throw himself at the feet of Jesus.

Perhaps prior to getting sick he'd studied the Torah and knew its prophecies about the coming Messiah, such as Isaiah 61:1: "The LORD has anointed me to bring good news to the poor; he has sent me to bind up the brokenhearted, to proclaim liberty to the captives, and the opening of the prison to those who are bound" (which Jesus quoted in Luke 4:18–19).

But perhaps his understanding of the prophecies had changed since he'd become a captive in his own body. Healthy Jews were longing for the Messiah to bring relief from the Roman occupation and heavy taxation—they assumed that liberty for captives meant freedom from the Roman Empire. But despite living in a conquered land, they still got to go home after work, eat at their own table, and watch their children grow up. But this man, this broken soul now living out his years in isolation, maybe he'd come to understand what the prophecies actually meant—that the Messiah's purpose was much more personal than anyone yet knew.

Whatever his story, something drove him past the law that required him to stay back, past the wall of disbelief that he could ever be restored, past the fear that the preacher man would shun him too.

"Lord, if you will, you can make me clean," he said (Luke 5:12).

So Jesus "stretched out his hand and touched him, saying, 'I will; be clean.' And immediately the leprosy left him" (v. 13).

The best part of the story isn't the healing that took place, though the healing was awesome. And it isn't the faith of the man, though he's an example for us to follow. The best part is when Jesus reached out His hand

and touched him. Because Jesus could've just spoken the words; instead He moved in and bent low to touch a man who no one had been willing to touch for a very long time. He touched him before he was clean. So while the words of healing restored his body, no doubt Jesus' touch restored his soul.

PRAYER FOCUS

Thank God for making you clean (today's entry is a reminder of why our prayers need to include gratitude, hmm?) and ask Him to give you His heart for the unclean.

MOVING FORWARD

o What part of your soul needs Jesus' healing touch?

o What's holding you back from the kind of bold faith the leper had?

o How can you connect with people in your life who aren't part of the "in" crowd, as Jesus did?

RISE

When [Jesus] returned to Capernaum after some days, it was reported that he was at home. And many were gathered together, so that there was no more room, not even at the door. And he was preaching the word to them. And they came, bringing to him a paralytic carried by four men. And when they could not get near him because of the crowd, they removed the roof above him, and when they had made an opening, they let down the bed on which the paralytic lay. And when Jesus saw their faith, he said to the paralytic, "Son, your sins are forgiven."

MARK 2:1–5

What a wild scene. There was such a mob at the house where Jesus was staying that latecomers couldn't get in, let alone be healed. Here was a guy paralyzed and strapped to a stretcher, and the people wouldn't make way. Tough crowd. They didn't even clear a path when they saw men dragging him onto the roof, a task that couldn't have been quick or smooth. When they finally made it up, they began hacking away at the straw and mud.

Jump-cut to inside the house. People surrounded Jesus while He preached and healed, but they were interrupted by the sounds of footsteps, dragging, and digging above them. And then chunks of the roof fell to the floor and probably on the heads of many in the room—but it worked. Jesus was moved by the faith that drove them to such heights (cheesy pun), and He forgave the paralytic.

Wait—wait! Um thanks, Jesus, but when we decided to scale the walls of this house, we were hoping for a real miracle … something along the lines of "rise and walk."

At least that's how it usually works. We go to Jesus with our own ideas about what He should do for us, and we're disappointed when He doesn't stick to the script. But it's often in the unexpected that Jesus does His best work.

Now some of the scribes were sitting there, questioning in their hearts, "Why does this man speak like that? He is blaspheming! Who can forgive sins but God alone?" And immediately Jesus, perceiving in his spirit that they questioned within themselves, said to them, "Why do you question these things in your hearts? Which is easier, to say to the paralytic, 'Your sins are forgiven,' or to say, 'Rise, take up your bed and walk'? But that you may know the Son of Man has authority on earth to forgive sins"—he said to the paralytic—"I say to you, rise, pick up your bed, and go home." And he rose and immediately picked up his bed and went out before them all, so that they were all amazed and glorified God, saying, "We never saw anything like this!" (Mark 2:6–12)

Christ's mission was to save souls, and healing was useful in demonstrating His power to do that. But it wasn't the mission. Healing displayed His compassion, love, and desire to restore, but it paled in comparison to His true purpose: to rescue and raise lost souls. Of course Jesus was able to discern the genuine faith of the men on the roof, along with the lack of faith of the crowd in the room. He exposed their thoughts—also a miracle—and announced His power to both heal and forgive. Since forgiveness is necessary to have a restored relationship with God and thus spend eternity with Him, Jesus was offering something far better than healing. So for the man who entered the room through the roof, walking was hopefully just the beginning of a lifetime spent following hard after the one who forgave him.

So that you may know I have the power to forgive, rise and walk.

Of course he did rise and walk, and this time probably through the front door.

PRAYER FOCUS

Thank God for forgiving your sins and then ask Him to give you the same kind of reckless faith and passion as the friends of the paralytic.

MOVING FORWARD

o In order to take such extreme measures, what must the four men carrying their friend have believed about Jesus?

o What keeps you from pursuing Jesus with that kind of passion?

o If you struggle to value spiritual growth over material, list three to five reasons spiritual growth matters more.

BLIND EYE

On another Sabbath, [Jesus] entered the synagogue
and was teaching, and a man was there whose right
hand was withered. And the scribes and the Pharisees
watched [Jesus], to see whether he would heal on the
Sabbath, so that they might find a reason to accuse him.

LUKE 6:6–7

What a strange, legalistic, and impersonal world. The
Pharisees were far more concerned about rules than
people. Here was a man whose hand was "withered,"
which means nerve damage and atrophy—a result of
what, we don't know. Regardless, he was missing the use
of his hand in a day and age when manual labor was
necessary to provide for oneself, not to mention a family.

In short, his need was great. And obvious to
onlookers.

Yet the religious leaders saw past him to Jesus—the object of their chagrin. This poor deformed man who had a name, a story, fear about the future, and probably hunger pain was just a pawn and a potential opportunity to trap the man derailing their world.

And Jesus *was* derailing their world. Instead of waiting with bated breath to hear the Pharisees speak, people were now flocking to the man from Nazareth who continually bent the rules, which made Him far more interesting and accessible to the people than the religious leaders ever were. He was unassuming and meek, yet authoritative and confident. And articulate. All while doing things no one else could do like healing ailments, driving out demons, and refusing to cower in the presence of the powerful.

So people flocked to Him, and He didn't disappoint.

> But [Jesus] knew their thoughts, and he said to the man with the withered hand, "Come and stand here." And he rose and stood there. And Jesus said to them, "I ask you, is it lawful on the Sabbath to do good or to do harm, to save life or to destroy it?" And after looking around at them all he said to him, "Stretch out your hand." And he did so, and his hand was restored. But

[the Pharisees] were filled with fury and
they discussed what they might do to Jesus.
(Luke 6:8–11)

It's easy to find fault with the Pharisees. They really
could be awful, and in a few words Jesus publicly outed
them for it. But lest we become just like them in self-
righteousness and self-involvement, consider how most
of us are like them. Think about the homeless people we
avoid making eye contact with as they hold cardboard
signs near traffic lights. And the understaffed soup
kitchens, under attended mission trips, and underfunded
relief organizations.

Let's be honest: Most of the time it's easier to ignore
the need. Our hearts are in fact calloused from exposure
to so much of it; we often don't give needy people a
second thought. Sometimes we feel annoyed and even
put upon. *Another person at another light*, we think.
How much loose change am I expected to carry? And yes,
like the Pharisees, we sometimes feel resentment toward
those we accuse of trying to "make us feel guilty."

But like the man with the withered hand, they
have names and stories. They have fears about the future
and hunger pain. Never mind the possible reasons why
their need is great—their need is obvious. And like the
Pharisees, we have much to learn from the Nazarene
who never turned a blind eye.

PRAYER FOCUS

Thank God He didn't turn His eyes from your need, repent of when you've behaved like a Pharisee, and ask Him for the same heart for the needy as Christ had.

MOVING FORWARD

o Obviously we can't respond to every need, but think of a time you could have but didn't. Why did you turn away? How would you handle it now if you got a second chance?

o Why did Jesus respond to needy people the way He did? What do you think He saw when He looked at them?

o List some ways you could react to obvious need in the future, in addition to giving money. That answer is too easy.

POOR

The people all tried to touch him, because power was coming from him and healing them all. Looking at his disciples, he said: "Blessed are you who are poor, for yours is the kingdom of God."

LUKE 6:19–20 NIV

No doubt, some of the crowds following Jesus brought with them a heavy dose of chaos. The most broken of humanity were coming out in droves. Logistically, there wasn't exactly a color-coded triage system in play, or roped-off lines with turnstiles to help with crowd control. It was an unmitigated free-for-all. It was a totally new kind of thing, for the desperate and for the disciples.

Moreover, there was an obvious relational disconnect. The disciples clearly didn't view the people the same way Jesus did. They were all in when it came to following Jesus, but learning to love and serve His chosen was another matter. That would take time.

One day before ministering to the crowd, Jesus called a time-out and sat down with His disciples. It was the perfect opportunity to chat about His kingdom perspective regarding the growing mob of poor people following them around. He kicked off His teaching with, "Blessed are you who are poor, for yours is the kingdom of God" (Luke 6:20). In other words: *That mess over there, fellas—it's beautiful. And guess what? They're not so different from you.*

Jesus explained the new pecking order: an upside-down system where the first would be last and the last would be first. All those broken folks were now the VIPs of God's kingdom. They were blessed. Fortunate. And better off than the most well-educated, able-bodied elite. Not because they were financially poor and physically diseased, but because their desperation made them humble and open to all that Jesus had to offer.

The rich were certainly invited, but few of them were poor enough in spirit to receive. Humility is found in low places, and Jesus didn't just tolerate or pity the desperate and chaotic crowds; He delighted in their humility. He esteemed them and came to revive their hearts and heal their bodies.

The disciples slowly but surely began to grasp that

far beyond the physical healings, the promises of God toward the poor were staggering. Eternal. Many of those who were coming out in droves—the most broken of humanity—were leaving healed and blessed, heirs in the kingdom of the Most High.

This was the new thing, the unmitigated free-for-all of Christ's love.

> This is what the high and exalted One says—he who lives forever, whose name is holy: "I live in a high and holy place, but also with him who is contrite and lowly in spirit, to revive the spirit of the lowly and to revive the heart of the contrite." (Isaiah 57:15)

PRAYER FOCUS

Ask God to make you "contrite and lowly in spirit" so you can experience revival.

MOVING FORWARD

o Put yourself in the disciples' shoes. Would it be difficult for you to minister to the desperate crowds? Why or why not?

o Is there someone you know who fits the "poor in spirit" category especially well? What attributes come to mind?

o What are ways you can pursue being "poor in spirit"?

PRESENCE, PART 1

One Sabbath, [Jesus] was going through the grain fields, and as they made their way, his disciples began to pluck heads of grain. And the Pharisees were saying to him, "Look, why are they doing what is not lawful [to do] on the Sabbath?"

MARK 2:23–24

Law 101. It actually was not unlawful to pluck a head of grain on the Sabbath. God commanded that His people rest every seventh day, and Moses specified that no fire be lit in its observance, so the Jews prepared their Shabbat food ahead of time. There was also ceremonial law that prohibited stuff, all of which fell into three main categories: no food prep, no making clothes or leather, and no building things.

But "no plucking" wasn't on any list. Leave it to the religious leaders to require more of the people than God did, at the expense of the Law's purpose. God wanted the Jews to rest because they spent their days doing physical labor, and the work was never done—for goodness' sake, they walked in the desert for forty years pulling their homes behind them. So the required rest wasn't for His sake but theirs, just as parents force exhausted little ones to take naps.

Back to the story.

> And [Jesus] said to them, "Have you never read what David did, when he was in need and was hungry, he and those who were with him: how he entered the house of God … and ate the bread of the Presence, which it is not lawful for any but the priests to eat, and also gave it to those who were with him?" (Mark 2:25–26)

History 101. In Old Testament times, the house of God (known as the tabernacle) was the place where God dwelled in the form of a cloud or pillar of fire. Besides His presence, there were only a few other things in the tent's two rooms.

First, a golden lampstand, made of solid gold and weighing seventy-five pounds, had six arms (think candelabra or menorah) with mini-lamps that burned continuously as the only source of light. Next, on the altar of incense—made from acacia wood, covered with gold, and standing three feet high—a special concoction burned twice a day. Finally, a small ornate table, also made from acacia wood and covered with gold, sat opposite the lampstand. On it the priests put twelve loaves of bread (think matzah or flatbread). The loaves were baked fresh and replaced each week, acknowledging God's constant presence with the Israelites—hence the name "bread of the Presence" (Exodus 25:30).

And all that to say, the daily rituals of lighting fires, burning incense, and baking bread were done to honor God's presence.

'Cause He was in the room.

Stick a pin in that.

Despite God's great favor toward David and his resulting victories on the battlefield, the guy could be a piece a work. He often let physical urges dictate his behavior, and this particular incident was no different. David was on King Saul's most wanted list, and he was tired, hungry, and on the run. So he racked up three violations:

1. David entered the house of God—a place where only priests were allowed to go.

2. David lied to the priest, telling him that he was on a secret mission from Saul. Nope.

3. David all but demanded to eat the bread of the Presence—food only priests were allowed to eat.

Ironically, the rule-obsessed Pharisees held David in the highest possible regard. But this new guy and His disciples with their heads-of-grain plucking—how dare they? As would become His habit, Jesus exposed the hypocrisy of their disgust and redirected the conversation to something far more disturbing.

To be continued.

PRAYER FOCUS

Ask God to reveal to you where you value rules over relationship.

MOVING FORWARD

o With all its pomp and circumstance, do you find talk of the tabernacle interesting or boring, and why?

o Imagine the room where God's presence dwelled. Imagine approaching the cloud or pillar of fire. How would standing in His presence, in that warm and quiet place, affect the way you view the requirements of the Law?

o Now imagine walking with Jesus. Imagine the unrestricted access, the casual conversation, and the warmth of His personality. That's all … just imagine.

PRESENCE, PART 2

"In the days of Abiathar the high priest, [David] entered the house of God and ate the consecrated bread, which is lawful only for priests to eat. And he also gave some to his companions." Then [Jesus] said to them, "The Sabbath was made for man, not man for the Sabbath. So the Son of Man is Lord even of the Sabbath."

MARK 2:25–28 NIV

The disciples were walking town to town with Jesus, listening to Him teach and watching Him heal. More than that, they were getting to know Him on a personal, intimate level. They were hanging out, telling stories, laughing, eating, and sleeping—they were communing with Him. I'm guessing the more time they spent with Jesus, the less anyone else's opinion of them mattered. Then again, the Pharisees had power, and there were consequences for breaking Sabbath law, like imprisonment and even death by stoning.

I imagine the moment of confrontation had a few of the disciples shaking in their sandals. Perhaps the hotheads were clenching their fists. Maybe a few were so sick of religious regulation they'd grown apathetic. Regardless, all disciple eyes were on Jesus as He stood His ground in the field of grain.

And then He took the ground and told them, "The Sabbath was made for man, not man for the Sabbath. So the Son of Man is lord even of the Sabbath" (Mark 2:27–28).

Two sentences that were not great for Pharisee relations.

"The Sabbath was made for man" (v. 27) meant that one of God's purposes in creating the Law was to bless. He wanted people to rest and refuel, to spend time with family and friends, and to be intentional about remembering His blessings, provision, and constant presence (#selfcare). The Sabbath was intended to be life-giving and in harmony with its first observance— the day God rested after creating all life. Conversely, "not man for the Sabbath" (v. 27) meant that man was not supposed to be burdened by the rule, as if serving it. God simply desired communion with His people, void of the tasks that distracted them during the week. He wanted them to be present with Him, and for them to be more aware of His presence with them—the basic requirements for any healthy relationship.

But then the conversation got dicey.

"So the Son of Man is lord even of the Sabbath" (v. 28). Up until that point, perhaps a few of the Pharisees were tracking with Jesus. Lest we impugn Kind David, perhaps this plucking thing isn't worth our time. And He's right that God made the Sabbath for our good. Since these men were just eating and not cooking, we've probably bitten off a little more than we can chew here, no pun intended. Wait ... did He just imply that *He's* Lord of the Sabbath?

Yep. Jesus repeatedly referred to Himself as the Son of Man, a reference not lost on the prophecy experts He was talking to—it's how Daniel referred to the coming Messiah in sixth century BC (Daniel 7:13). And now Jesus used it to refer to Himself and assert the only logical conclusion: He is Lord (i.e., He rules over the Sabbath). First David, then Daniel; it was a one-two Old Testament punch that threw the Pharisees off balance enough to end the exchange right there. For the time being anyway.

Here's the irony. These Pharisees' regulations, which protected the tabernacle pomp and circumstance they adhered to and the Sabbath rest they so keenly enforced, were all for the purpose of acknowledging and honoring God's presence. Yet standing in front of them was the one their lives revolved around, and they refused to see it. The disciples saw it. The needy crowds that came from far and wide saw it. But these men so close in proximity to Jesus, both physically and intellectually, somehow could not. Perhaps if they'd been more willing to set aside the distracting tasks of the day in exchange for more of God's presence, they would have.

'Cause He was in the room.

PRAYER FOCUS

Ask God to forgive you for when you've prioritized other things over His presence and ask Him for eyes to see Him when He's there.

MOVING FORWARD

o What do you prioritize over spending time in God's presence?

o In what area of your life are you rejecting Christ's Lordship?

o What is your favorite thing about spending time with God, and what do you need to change to be able to spend more time with Him?

LIGHT

"Whoever believes in [Jesus] is not condemned, but whoever does not believe is condemned already because, he has not believed in the name of the only Son of God. And this is the judgment: the light has come into the world, but people loved the darkness rather than the light because their works were evil."

JOHN 3:18–19

Nicodemus came to Jesus at night, to sit and talk and learn—and hide. John's Gospel doesn't specify that the meeting took place in the dark to keep his fellow Pharisees from seeing it, but Jesus' words implied as much. *Until you're willing to step out of the dark and into the light, you're not with me.*

But let's back up.

The passive-aggression of the Pharisees was

evolving into just plain aggression. The more Jesus taught and healed, the more He gained a reputation; and His audience was growing. Among the multitudes, there were some who believed Jesus was the long-awaited Savior and rightly so—He was repeatedly saying as much, which was why the Pharisees were no longer hiding their disdain. There were murder plots in the works and outright attempts on Jesus' life, but the religious leaders tried to keep their plans under wraps because they feared the reaction of His followers.

So it makes sense that Nicodemus, a renowned Pharisee with a reputation and career at stake, was scared to be seen with Jesus. Yet the first thing he said in his secret meeting was, "Rabbi, we know that you are a teacher come from God, for no one can do these signs that you do unless God is with him" (John 3:2). He was on the right track. Jesus came from God and His works were evidence of that. Typically, Pharisees were their own biggest fans; they were proud of their education, accomplishments, piousness, and zeal—and all of the above earned them status and power. That made it difficult for Nicodemus to know how to respond to the man who was clearly from God, and "teacher" was the highest praise he could muster.

But Nicodemus' statement didn't go far enough, and Jesus' response, while gentle, didn't pull any punches. Paraphrased, it went something like this:

Because I'm God's Son, whoever believes in me will have eternal life, and those who don't believe in me stand condemned—although my purpose in coming wasn't to condemn; it was to save. But unfortunately, Nicodemus, what you count as worthy of salvation—your resume, your position, your ambition, your good works—I count as evil because they are the very things keeping you from following me now.

Being unwilling to meet Jesus in the light of day was the picture of Nicodemus' unwillingness to follow, period. At least on that night. He didn't know it yet, but Nicodemus loved the darkness and all he'd built in its domain. It wasn't until after Jesus was crucified that the reticent Pharisee emerged from the shadows.

> Joseph of Arimathea, who was a disciple of Jesus, … came and took away his body. Nicodemus also, who earlier had come to Jesus by night, came bringing a mixture of myrrh and aloes, about seventy-five pounds in weight. They took the body of Jesus and bound it in linen cloths with the spices, as is the burial custom of the Jews. Now in the place where he was crucified there was a garden, and in the garden a new tomb in which no one had yet been laid. So because of the Jewish day of Preparation, since the

tomb was close at hand, they laid Jesus there. (John 19:38–42)

What caused the change? What made Nicodemus willing to publicly express his love for Jesus? Perhaps it was the unjust conviction at the hands of the Pharisees. Perhaps it was the viciousness of the Romans as they carried out the sentence. Perhaps it was the cheering of the crowd, the very ones Jesus taught and fed and healed. Most likely, it was the result of immense guilt— an attempt to make up for his previous cowardice. Whatever his reasons, the fear, pride, and disbelief that had kept Nicodemus in the dark no longer did.

"Awake, O sleeper, and arise from the dead, and Christ will shine on you" (Ephesians 5:14).

PRAYER FOCUS

If there's any part of your life where you're either hiding your passion for Christ, or hiding something shameful, ask God to light it.

MOVING FORWARD

o What have you risked to follow Jesus, and what price have you paid?

o In what ways is Christ like light? In what ways are people asleep?

o What in your life and heart are you still keeping in the dark, away from the sifting, transforming light of Jesus?

POWER

[Christ is] far above all rule and authority, power and dominion, and every name that is invoked, not only in the present age but also in the one to come.

EPHESIANS 1:21 NIV

Nicodemus and his Sanhedrin colleagues were the political and religious rule makers and enforcers of their day. They doled out a dizzying mess of statutes, down to the most impossible to follow, legalistic minutia. They were especially fond of legislating Sabbath observances, purity, and tithing laws.

Of course, the Pharisees created all kinds of loopholes for themselves. They deemed the mutable "oral law" to be equally as binding as the written one. In other words, they could change (or follow) a law however and whenever they saw fit. Consequently, this group of rule-maker-breakers was thought by the people to be high-handed, hypocritical Zealots. Their shameless arrogance provoked resentment and fear-based obedience.

They were, essentially, fancy bullies.

As far as he was concerned, Nicodemus deserved the glory he got. After all, his command of Scripture, religious training, prominence in the community, and the power to throw folks in jail for, say, fishing on the Sabbath, mandated it. And who would dare question him? What common man was more powerful than he?

Nicodemus discovered the answers when he met Jesus.

Jesus didn't look very important. He didn't adorn Himself with elaborate garments, phylacteries, and long tassels the way the Pharisees did. Nor did He brandish a list of credentials and demand deference. Yet His power defied and preempted all systems of institutional hierarchy.

His otherworldly authority was dispensed with compassion and grace. It was undeniable. Jesus cast out demons and did miracles. And Nicodemus was among the few men of power who knew what that meant: Jesus was sent by God.

And although His presence threatened Nicodemus' position, power, and livelihood, it beckoned his heart and compelled him to risk all he'd built. In

Jesus he found real truth and power, not the religious invention he was a part of. He found the Word; it had been made flesh and was dwelling among them (John 1:14). The body of Scripture Nicodemus had dedicated his entire life to knowing, knew him by name. He found the hope to which he'd been called.

And it was beyond powerful.

PRAYER FOCUS

Repent of the times you've valued status over humility, then ask God to bring you to your knees in gratitude and awe from the fact that He's in relationship with you.

MOVING FORWARD

o Write down a time when you felt better than someone else because of your religious status or choices, or their lack thereof.

o What's a rule or lifestyle choice you've stressed as important, perhaps at the expense of a more direct or pure connection with Jesus?

o We rarely have to risk a lot to follow Jesus. But what are some things you'd have a hard time risking to follow Jesus?

BELIEVE

For God so loved the world that he gave his one and only Son, that whoever believes in him shall not perish but have eternal life.

JOHN 3:16 NIV

A promise and a covenant are the same but different.

A promise is a declaration that something will or will not be done. A covenant is a contract, a formal agreement between two or more parties. In the Old Testament, God made promises in the form of covenants with ancient Israel.

Because it was His idea, because He is God, and because He knows what's good for His people, the covenant was on His terms and He established the conditions. God promised to protect the Israelites if they kept His law and remained faithful to Him.

But they didn't.

It was impossible. Not because God's plan was flawed but because His chosen people were. The covenant served to illustrate their desperate need for a perfect God. It was not designed to save them but to point to the one who could.

Enter the new covenant. Enter Jesus. Jesus is the new covenant. If you are born again, you will be saved. That is the new contract, the new formal agreement. And it tripped up Nicodemus something terrible.

Jesus explained, "Very truly I tell you, no one can see the kingdom of God unless they are born again" (John 3:3 NIV).

"How can someone be born when they are old?" Nicodemus asked, taking His words way too literally. "Surely they cannot enter a second time into their mother's womb to be born!" (v. 4).

The fact that Nicodemus was a Pharisee made his response that much dumber. Jesus pointed out that Nicodemus was a guy who'd dedicated his life to studying and teaching the old covenant, that the old covenant pointed to the new covenant, and that the new covenant was standing right in front of him—so Jesus was very clearly *not* talking about reentering his mother's womb, and maaaaybe Nicodemus should've been quicker on the uptake.

But he wasn't.

Flawed Nicodemus was stuck on the external. His life was all about outward pretentiousness, long-winded empty prayers, ridiculous outfits, and strong-arming the community. It was all fake. Actual faith was not part of Nicodemus' religious acumen. But he'd need it to believe this teacher who came from God, talking about flesh giving birth to flesh and the Spirit giving birth to spirit.

It's a heart thing, Nico. Heart, not works. It takes actual faith.

Representing the new covenant, Jesus Christ, was standing before him declaring the most extraordinary promise ever made: *If you are born again, you will see the kingdom of heaven. If you believe, you will not perish but have eternal life. I've already chosen you; now it's your turn to make the choice.*

Nicodemus, what say you?

PRAYER FOCUS

Thank God for freedom from the Law, but in response, ask Him to give you more faith and zeal.

MOVING FORWARD

o Is it sometimes difficult for you to believe the new covenant has replaced the old? Or do you still sometimes think following rules is more important?

o In what ways can you identify with Nicodemus?

o Describe the moment you knew there was a choice about Jesus to be made.

PERCEIVE

"The eye is the lamp of the body. If your eyes are healthy, your whole body will be full of light. But if your eyes are unhealthy, your whole body will be full of darkness. If then the light within you is darkness, how great is that darkness!"

MATTHEW 6:22–23 NIV

How you see is what you get. Life and death, light and darkness—you choose the outcome when you choose whom to follow. Let the ranger with the big flashlight lead you, and you'll get back to camp safely. Ignore the ranger with the big flashlight, and you'll become disoriented, lost, and eaten by a bear.

The choice is yours. Whichever route, it's your eyes that inform your body how to proceed; they communicate to your heart and soul which way to go.

Of course, no one who ignores the light thinks they'll end up as bear food. Their path is better, they believe, or at least easier. Regardless, they're unable to discern in the darkness that it leads straight into the bear cave. Jesus said, "I am the light of the world. Whoever follows me will never walk in darkness, but will have the light of life" (John 8:12 NIV). In effect, He told His listeners that if they wanted to make it out of the woods alive, they'd do well to follow the one with the flashlight.

The Pharisees were incensed by His claims. They asserted their unmatched knowledge of the woods and wanted to know who made Him ranger. They questioned Jesus about it while a crowd was listening, and based on His answers, many in the crowd believed Jesus was indeed the Light of the World. And because they made the choice to follow Him, they had the light.

That's how it works—in that order. When you choose to follow Him, you *have* the light because He *is* the Light. He's the one who gives you the ability to see the path and perceive your surroundings as they really are. There is no do-it-yourself home remedy for healthy eyes and right perception. Jesus is the only one who can make you see.

Once your eyes are healthy, everything is healthy because what you perceive affects your entire being. "If your eyes are healthy, your whole body will be full of light," Jesus said in Matthew 6:22 (NIV). Likewise, a doctor shines a bright light into an unconscious patient's eye to check for brain death. If the eye responds to the light and the pupil constricts, the patient's brain is okay. If it doesn't, it's dead.

But unlike the person with brain death, it's never too late to make the decision to follow the light. We can choose to respond to the one who chose us first. He is the Light. He knows the way and will lead us safely back to camp.

PRAYER FOCUS

Thank God for making your eyes healthy, but ask Him to help you never take that for granted and to always "see clearly."

MOVING FORWARD

o Describe when you first realized you could see and perceive clearly.

o How have your healthy eyes affected your whole body? In other words, how has your healthy perception of Christ affected your life in general?

o In what circumstances have you rejected the "ranger's flashlight," and what can you do to ensure that happens less frequently?

PRECIOUS

People were bringing little children to Jesus for him to place his hands on them, but the disciples rebuked them. When Jesus saw this, he was indignant. He said to them, "Let the little children come to me, and do not hinder them, for the kingdom of God belongs to such as these."

MARK 10:13–14 NIV

Sometimes the disciples were ridiculous. No doubt some of the children who were brought to Jesus needed to be healed—the whole point was for Jesus to lay hands on them, something parents of sick kids would be desperate to do. So not only were the disciples saying no to kids coming forward, but they were likely saying no to sick kids as well.

Not exactly a Make-A-Wish moment.

And Jesus was indignant, which revealed His heart toward them. To keep Jesus from precious little people, to hinder access to Him in any way, provoked His righteous anger. Because not only were the children vulnerable and in need—they were the exact representation of those He came to save.

"The kingdom of God belongs to such as these" (Mark 10:14 NIV).

Children are simple. They're appropriately awestruck by the world around them. They're wide-eyed and expectant and moldable and trusting. By nature they aren't jaded or judgmental—those qualities come with age, along with self-focus, self-reliance, self-protection, self-promotion, and self-praise. On the contrary, children (most of them, anyway) are willing to defer and to receive, to climb into the Savior's lap and be cared for, to be led and loved on.

The children approached Jesus in a way we're supposed to emulate.

"'Truly I tell you, anyone who will not receive the kingdom of God like a little child will never enter it.' And he took the children in his arms, placed his hands on them and blessed them" (Mark 10:15–16).

Jesus rebuked the disciples for putting restrictions on access to Him, and the same goes for us. Our preconceived ideas about how relationship with God works, and our lofty opinions about how it *should* work, restrict our ability to receive all He has for us. Our religious merit systems restrict us—we'd rather earn our way onto His lap. Our disappointments, bitterness, and defensiveness restrict us. Our shame and guilt and insecurity restrict us. Our pride in our appearance and accomplishments restricts us. Our desire to control our lives restricts us. All of it keeps us from coming unhindered to the one who counts us precious.

The children went to Jesus without anything of value to offer Him except their love and excitement to be there. He wanted to spend time with them, hug them, and heal them. He *wanted* to. And we are precious to Jesus too when we recognize our need for His help, when we're willing to defer, to receive, to be led, and to be loved on. We're precious when we come to Jesus with the simple expectation that because of who He is and how He loves, we're welcome, wanted, forgiven, and will be restored.

PRAYER FOCUS

In the spirit of childlike faith, go ahead and pray some popular children's prayers, but really mean them.

MOVING FORWARD

- o What are some of the restrictions you've placed on your relationship with Jesus? What hinders you from communing with Him more closely?

- o Read Isaiah 43:1–4, Luke 12:6–7, and Romans 5:6–8. According to His Word, what does God see when He looks at you?

- o What are some new habits and thought patterns you need to develop in order to approach God in a more precious, faith-like-a-child way?

SET FREE,
PART 1

Now he was teaching in one of the synagogues on the Sabbath. And behold, there was a woman who had had a disabling spirit for eighteen years. She was bent over and could not fully straighten herself. When Jesus saw her, he called her over and said to her, "Woman, you are freed from your disability." And he laid his hands on her, and immediately she was made straight, and she glorified God. But the ruler of the synagogue, indignant because Jesus had healed on the Sabbath, said to the people, "There are six days in which work ought to be done. Come on those days and be healed, and not on the Sabbath day." Then the Lord answered him, "You hypocrites! Does not each of you on the Sabbath untie his ox or his donkey from the manger and lead it away to water it? And ought not this woman, a daughter of Abraham whom Satan bound for eighteen years, be loosed from this bond on the Sabbath day?"

Reporter: Ladies, thank you for being here. As part of our "Where Are They Now?" series, we're catching up with women involved in healings that captivated the region. I'd like to talk about your unique encounters with Jesus and how those moments have changed your lives. Daughter of Abraham, let's start with you. Tell us about that fateful day in the temple. Do you recall what He was teaching?

Daughter of Abraham: I remember *how* He was teaching—with such power and authority it made me question if the other teachers knew anything at all. I was captivated by His words and trying to twist my body enough to look at Him, but I couldn't. That's when He saw me and called me forward.

Reporter: Were you fearful?

Daughter of Abraham: Not fearful, but certainly surprised. Being addressed by a man in public was unexpected. And everyone watching me was a little unnerving, but I was never fearful. I was eager to get to Jesus. It took a minute because of my condition, you know.

Reporter: How did the congregation respond?

Daughter of Abraham: Shocked quiet. Then Jesus interrupted the silence with, "Woman, you are set free from your infirmity." And He put His hand on me.

Reporter: That's when you straightened up?

Daughter of Abraham: Yes, immediately. Jesus was the first person I'd stood face-to-face with in nearly two decades. I began praising God like nobody's business!

Reporter: I heard the synagogue leader did not share your enthusiasm.

Daughter of Abraham: Ha! No. He threw a fit about healing on the Sabbath, but Jesus put him in his place. It was pretty great.

Reporter: Jesus gave you the exclusive moniker "daughter of Abraham." I'd say that's a pretty big deal. How did you feel when He said that?

Daughter of Abraham: Elated. Jubilant. Ecstatic. But there's not an accurate enough word. By calling me daughter of Abraham, He was informing everyone in the synagogue that women have the same spiritual status as men. We are equal in the kingdom. Honestly, it was every bit as remarkable as standing up straight, if not more.

Reporter: How has your life changed since that day?

Daughter of Abraham: Oh, you know, just in every conceivable way. He chose me. Me. In a single moment, He healed my body and assigned my God-given identity. I still marvel at each word that was said, what He did, and what it all meant.

Reporter: Which is?

Daughter of Abraham: I am chosen and have been set free.

PRAYER FOCUS

Take your vices to God, anything that's got hold of your heart more than it should, and ask God to help free you from it.

MOVING FORWARD

o What's a name you would want Jesus to give you?

o If Jesus showed up at your church and called you to Himself, what would He want to set you free from?

o What are some steps you can start taking to be freed from whatever vice has held you in bondage?

SET FREE, PART 2

She had heard the reports about Jesus and came up behind him in the crowd and touched his garment. For she said, "If I touch even his garments, I will be made well." And immediately the flow of blood dried up, and she felt in her body that she was healed of her disease. And Jesus, perceiving in himself that power had gone out from him, immediately turned about in the crowd and said, "Who touched my garments?" And his disciples said to him, "You see the crowd pressing around you, and yet you say, 'Who touched me?'" And he looked around to see who had done it. But the woman, knowing what had happened to her, came in fear and trembling and fell down before him and told him the whole truth. And he said to her, "Daughter,

your faith has made you well; go in peace, and be
healed of your disease."

MARK 5:27–34

Reporter: Woman with the Issue of Blood, your healing
transpired under quite different circumstances. Tell us
about your encounter with Jesus.

Daughter: For the record, I go by "Daughter"
now. Like Daughter of Abraham, I was afflicted for a
long time—twelve years. I'd been to numerous doctors,
and no one could help me. I was desperate.

Reporter: Desperate enough to risk the crowd?

Daughter: Yes, I had to. It was the only way I
could get to Jesus. I knew there was a good possibility
of being recognized and severely punished. Being
ceremonially unclean is not a casual offense, you know.
I'd been banned from all human contact, but I had to try.

Reporter: And there you are being pushed around
in a throng of people. Tell us about the moment—the
touch that has captivated the hearts and imaginations of
believers everywhere. You were healed right then?

Daughter: Yes. Immediately. It felt as if His
entire being, even His cloak, was saturated with God's
miraculous power. The bleeding stopped. I could feel in
my body that I was free from my suffering.

Reporter: I imagine you were hoping to slip

back through the crowd undetected, but that's not what happened, is it?

Daughter: Not at all. Jesus turned around to the crowd and asked, "Who touched my clothes?" At first, I froze. I didn't know if He was angry or not. But He kept looking. I realized, *Of course He'll know it's me. He's Jesus. His cloak alone just healed me.* So I came forward and fell at His feet.

Reporter: I'll ask you the same question I asked Daughter of Abraham: Were you fearful?

Daughter: The circumstances were certainly frightening. I was trembling when I told Him the truth, but after a few moments, I wasn't fearful of Him. His eyes were full of compassion. He could have kept going on His way, but He stopped to acknowledge me, not rebuke me. He listened and was sympathetic to my suffering. He said, "Daughter, your faith has healed you. Go in faith and be freed from your suffering."

Reporter: How has your life changed since that day?

Daughter: Well, obviously I'm physically healed, but my healing didn't eliminate my need for Jesus—it connected me to it. He set me free to pursue my life in Him. The very thing satan tried to destroy me with, Jesus used to restore our relationship and make me whole in every way. I am chosen and set free.

PRAYER FOCUS

That prayer you prayed from the previous entry? Keep going with it. Keep bringing your vices to God and ask Him to free you from them. It's okay to be desperate.

MOVING FORWARD

o What are you willing to risk to get to Jesus?

o Describe a time when you felt desperate to be in His presence. What did you do?

o How has Jesus restored the parts of your life that satan has tried to use to destroy you?

CREATED

For we are his workmanship, created in Christ Jesus
for good works, which God prepared beforehand, that
we should walk in them.

EPHESIANS 2:10

Why bother creating something?

Why invent that specific widget when there's a sort-of-close-but-not-quite version at the local superstore? What's the point of painting an original when countless reproductions abound? Why open the specialty coffee shop you've been dreaming of when dozens of franchises dot the landscape?

Why build or make something when it's so much easier to just … not?

Good question. Especially after weighing risk against reward and imagining a few worst-case scenarios. It takes all of five seconds to see that creating something meaningful can be costly and complicated.

So how is it worth it?

Ask an inventor, an artist, or an entrepreneur, and they'll tell you that it just is. They'll tell you it's not solely about the finished product. They'll describe the joy of the process—the satisfaction attained through brainstorming, problem solving, implementing, growing, and improving. They'll light up as they break down the unexpected discoveries made along the way, like the prize of persevering and the incredible new avenues through which they can give and love.

Ask the Creator Himself, and He will tell you the same. It's worth it. He paid the cost and knows our reward. He is greater than any worst-case scenario. Read His Word, and you'll discover that He created you, formed you, redeemed you, and called you by name. He'll tell you He has a plan for your life and that you're not a discount, sort-of-close-but-not-quite version of anyone else. You are you, and you have a specific purpose. His entire collection contains not a single reproduction. And despite how crowded this planet can sometimes feel, your life proves you need to exist. It also confirms there are good works for you to do.

Because we are made in God's image, we're created to dream, create, serve, love, and walk in the things He created in advance for us to do. The discovery and progression of it all is for our good and His glory. It's a big deal. It's where we catch the most life-changing glimpses of who He is and who we are in Him.

Look at Peter, Matthew, and the rest of the gang. Before Jesus ever called them by name, God had already purposed every single event we read in our Bibles today. They were chosen. Their good works were already prepared. Their job was to walk them out.

Lest we get hung up on the grandiosity of their calling and deem ourselves losers by comparison, remember that we're chosen to do the same thing: to further the kingdom and create disciples. God has already created the unique ways through which we can fulfill the Great Commission. Our job is to actually go for it.

Wonderfully, that can happen anytime and anywhere—in a machine shop, a painting class, or the corner table in your specialty coffee shop.

PRAYER FOCUS

Ask God to reveal to you how you can maximize your calling and discover the "good works" God created us to do.

MOVING FORWARD

o Describe a meaningful work you've been a part of.

o What did you learn about God throughout the process?

o What unique opportunities can you create to further the kingdom?

WOLVES

"Watch out for false prophets.
They come to you in sheep's clothing,
but inwardly they are ferocious wolves."

MATTHEW 7:15 NIV

Wolves are not detected because of inferior costume design. On the contrary, they know their craft and dress themselves accordingly. They've studied the trends and understand the importance of adapting to the sheep's ever-changing preferences and desires. Solid branding is key, and lucky for the wolf, it's never been easier.

Wolves know what to capitalize on. Instant gratification makes the short list. Also, pithy tweets and expertly filtered memes can eclipse actual Bible knowledge any day of the week. Social responsibility? Always a boon for business. And, of course, being your best you. Or just being you. #selfie #selflove #selfcare #selfselfself

Wolves appeal to the masses. They're not hawking dissension or controversy—that would be crazy. Controversy might sustain a second-rate blog, but it's not going to fill stadiums. Unity, inspiration, and goodwill are what pay dividends and sell a sick amount of swag. #chaching

Oh yeah, and it makes the world a better place and whatnot. "Who are we to judge anything or anyone?" the wolf says, hoping to counteract any possible discernment. "We're just here to spread the love and be awesome." #imustincrease #followmemore #isaywhatyouwanttohear

Unity, used cars, timeshares, spirituality—it makes no difference, they're all just products. And like any salesman worth his salt, the wolf knows the product better than the consumers do. He relies on his creativity, messaging, branding, and personality. Sure, Jesus is discussed, but mostly in an anecdotal sort of way, not in the He-is-Messiah-the-Son-of-the-Living-God sort of way. That would make Jesus the headliner and bad for business. Wolves draw attention to themselves, their names, their products—and, most destructively, their take on goodness and love—with narratives far more on trend than the dusty words of yesteryear.

Wolves use all possible means to satisfy their

hunger for recognition, honor, status, and wealth. And in a time when vainglorious behavior is celebrated, and selfish-ambition looks like high-energy do-gooding, wolves have become harder to detect.

But detect we must, lest we be deceived.

So how do we do that? For starters, we quit consuming. We stop opting for one-off Jesus stories and spiritual inspiration and go directly to the inspired Word of God. We read His stories and meditate on His words. We replace instant gratification with long-term soul satisfaction by allowing Christ to determine our preferences and desires. We reject any message promising ease or lack of resistance as contrary to Jesus' example and message. We learn who He is and who we are in Him—we are chosen. Not by wolves to be exploited, but chosen by the true and living God, to be with Him now and for all of eternity.

PRAYER FOCUS

Ask God to give you discernment in recognizing wolves or messages from wolves.

MOVING FORWARD

o Jesus said, "By their fruit you will recognize them" (Matthew 7:16 NIV). What does that mean?

o How can you improve your wolf-spotting skills?

o What measures can you take to guard your heart and mind and loved ones from wolves?

WELLSPRING

[Jesus] came to a town of Samaria called Sychar. …
Jacob's well was there; so Jesus, wearied as he was
from his journey, was sitting beside the well. It was
about the sixth hour. A woman from Samaria came to
draw water. Jesus said to her, "Give me a drink." …
[But she] said to him, "How is it that you, a Jew, ask
for a drink from me, a woman of Samaria?" (For Jews
have no dealings with Samaritans.) Jesus answered
her, "If you knew the gift of God, and who it is that is
saying to you, 'Give me a drink,' you would have asked
him, and he would have given you living water."

JOHN 4:5–10

It was high noon in Samaria, and Jesus was talking
to a woman. The moment was remarkable because

Jews typically hated Samaritans. The offspring of intermarriage, which Jewish law prohibited, they were a nation of people who were half Jew, half Gentile and therefore wholly despised. In fact, even though Samaria was located in between, when traveling from Judea to Galilee, Jews added days to their journey by walking clear around it.

But not Jesus.

Also remarkable was the timing, because water was always drawn in the morning when the sun was still low. The well was on the outskirts of town, and the work was arduous. Drawing water at noon in the desert heat was a clear sign this woman was avoiding people—and Jesus knew why.

> Jesus said to her, "Go, call your husband, and come here." The woman answered him, "I have no husband." Jesus said to her, "You are right in saying, 'I have no husband'; for you have had five husbands, and the one you now have is not your husband. What you have said is true." (John 4:16–18)

Her reputation preceded her, probably everywhere she went. She'd been used and tossed away; or maybe she was in the habit of tossing men away. Whatever the reason, her life was wrought with scandal and void of friendship, and I can only imagine what the townspeople said behind her back. Or maybe to her face. Which made what came next the most remarkable of all.

"The woman said to him, 'I know that Messiah is coming (he who is called Christ). When he comes, he will tell us all things.' Jesus said to her, 'I who speak to you am he'" (v. 26).

Those seven words, spoken to the least likely of humans, changed the course of history:

I who speak to you am He.

Until that moment, Jesus had only implied His true identity. The actual words—the announcement of God's arrival on earth, the fulfillment of hundreds of years of messianic prophecy, the Master's plan to restore the whole of creation—were whispered to the one no one wanted. He knew she'd be there. He knew her name and her pain and her need. *She was, in fact, the reason He came,* because from the well of Christ's immense and indiscriminating mercy flows His mission:

To rescue and redeem the lost.

"Whoever drinks of the water that I give them will never thirst. Indeed, the water I give them will become in them a spring of water welling up to eternal life" (v. 14 NIV).

PRAYER FOCUS

Ask God to completely rid you of any prejudice toward anyone so that you see them as Christ saw the Samaritan woman, then ask Him to help you value living water over physical needs.

MOVING FORWARD

- o What kind of statement was Jesus making by choosing to announce Himself to an outcast who was both a Samaritan and a woman?

- o How was Jesus different than every other person she'd come across? How was she expecting to be treated by Him?

- o After she realized Jesus was the Messiah, she spread the word. How can you do the same?

MISSION

"'I was hungry and you gave me food, I was thirsty and you gave me drink, I was a stranger and you welcomed me, I was naked and you clothed me, I was sick and you visited me, I was in prison and you came to me.' Then the righteous will answer Jesus, saying, 'Lord, when did we see you hungry and feed you, or thirsty and give you drink? And when did we see you a stranger and welcome you, or naked and clothe you? And when did we see you sick or in prison and visit you?' And the King will answer them, 'Truly, I say to you, as you did it to one of the least of these my brothers, you did it to me.'"

MATTHEW 25:35–40

Jesus chose twelve men to be the original gospel task force. Twelve disciples who traveled with Him for three years, watched Him minister to crowds, and listened to Him teach, all the while learning about God's heart toward people. Because after Jesus ascended to heaven, those twelve men would be charged with His mission: to tell the world the good news that relationship with God can be restored. That heaven awaits the followers of Jesus. That anyone who believes Jesus is God's Son will be saved. And that following Jesus means loving God and people the way He did: the lepers who were social outcasts; the blind and lame who were societal burdens; the women and servants who were marginalized and disenfranchised; the children who were vulnerable and overlooked; the well to-do who were hopelessly self-sufficient; the prodigals, the broken, and the bent. They all shared the same need—their total inability to rescue themselves.

Jesus came to seek and save the lost.

The disciples underwent a massive recalibration. Everything they thought they knew about how to live turned upside down. The new kingdom order would be to put others first, to love when people hate, to pray for those who persecute, to lead by serving, to give when it costs, to trust in God's provision no matter how glaring the lack, and to die in order to live. Jesus changed everything, and sharing His love, life, and purpose with all people, including the least of these—especially the least of these—became the disciples' sole mission.

More than two thousand years later, the mission remains. Christ followers are still building the kingdom of God, and we can partake in the process; we are, in fact, called to it. We still must rescue and lead people to the one who made them, loves them, can heal them and restore them. There is a war being waged—darkness verses light—and to participate in God's sure victory, we must be fearless in our self-denial and bold in telling the truth. We must be tenacious in our faith that God will be faithful to His word and His work. We must love those He loves, serve those He serves, and refuse to relent in doing the good Jesus did. And all for His sake because He loves us, because He rescued us, and because we love Him back. And until He returns, the mission will remain.

Cue the cool music and slow-motion walk. God's chosen are on the move.

PRAYER FOCUS

Thank God for His Son, thank Him for not only sending Jesus to die but also showing you how to live, and ask Him for the courage to live out what you're learning about Him.

MOVING FORWARD

o Jesus takes what you do and don't do for others personally. What does that mean to you? How does it motivate you?

o Who comes to mind when you read Matthew 25:35–40? What is the Holy Spirit leading you to do?

o Our mission is clear, but we're easily distracted. What in your life, your relationships, your priorities, your perspective needs to change in order for you to be more active in Christ's mission?

ABOUT THE AUTHORS

Amanda Jenkins is a speaker and author, having written four books, including *Confessions of a Raging Perfectionist*, a memoir that has inspired women's Bible studies and conferences all over the country. She specializes in writing and teaching raw authenticity in our faith, which was the intent behind this devotional. She lives in Chicago with her husband, Dallas, and four children.

Kristen Hendricks is an author, artist, and the creator of *Small Girl Design*. Before illustrating (literally) how a Big God can work through a Small Girl, Kristen witnessed this truth time and again during her tenure as executive director of an anti-trafficking organization in East Africa. Kristen lives in the Chicago area with her two daughters and husband, Joe, where she strives to champion for women and point them to Christ.

Dallas Jenkins has been a filmmaker for over twenty years and is also a sought-after speaker, blogger, and media guest on pop culture and faith topics. He's produced or directed over a dozen films, including *What If ...* and *The Resurrection of Gavin Stone*. The viral success of his short films about the Gospels from a different perspective led to his current series, *The Chosen*, and this devotional.